Brassey's *History of Uniforms*

Brassey's *History of Uniforms*

English Civil War

By Philipp J.C. Elliot-Wright

Colour plates by Christa Hook

Series editor Tim Newark

For my long suffering wife Caz.

First English Edition 1997

UK editorial offices: Brassey's Ltd, 33 John Street, London
WC1N 2AT
UK Orders: Marston Book Services, PO Box 269, Abingdon,
OX14 4SD

North American Orders: Brassey's Inc,
PO Box 960, Herndon, VA 22070, USA

Philipp J.C. Elliot-Wright has asserted his moral right to be
identified as the author of this work.

Library of Congress Cataloging in Publication Data available
British Library Cataloguing in Publication Data
A catalogue record for this book is available from the British
Library

ISBN 1 8575 3 211 2 Hardcover

Typeset by Harold Martin & Redman Ltd.
Originated, printed and bound in Singapore
under the supervisison of M.R.M. Graphics Ltd,
Winslow, Buckinghamshire.

Contents

Introduction

The stereotypical vision of the conflicts that were fought out during the 1640s and 50s is of enthusiastic amateurs, with a few returned mercenaries, fighting in clothes which identified their respective cause. The very words Cavalier and Roundhead still conjure up images of gaudily apparelled, long haired Royalists and sombrely attired, crop haired Parliamentarians. These associations come largely from contemporary propaganda and in reality, the various wars which raged across England, Scotland, Ireland and overseas saw armies that were part and parcel of the age's developing military science. Far from being fought by civilians in uniform who blundered their way to some form of competence, the respective armies were raised from the first by professional military officers educated in the most up to date concepts of the harsh school of the Thirty Years War. Whilst it took a while to provide the appropriate standards of weapons and equipment, by 1643 the combatants had established efficient wartime economies able to supply the bulk of their needs. With respect to those needs, the ever more dominant role being played by gunpowder and firepower ensured uniforms and equipment progressively evolved during the 1640s and 1650s to reflect the changing tactical and technological parameters.

On the eve of the First Bishop's War in early 1639 the raising of an English military establishment appeared little changed from that which had been mobilised to stop the Armada some fifty years before There was no standing army as such, the landed magnates of each county being relied upon, in almost feudal style, to produce soldiers. Yet the army which so ineffectively marched north to confront the Scots did so generally organised, drilled and equipped to the most modern of contemporary European standards. In fact, the product of the first part of this period, the Bishop's Wars, the revolt in Ireland and the Civil War, was England's first standing army, the New Model Army. Ultimately, the 1650s saw this professional force fight in a variety of theatres of conflict, the Highlands of Scotland, the wetlands of Ireland, the tropical Caribbean and the traditional fields of Flanders. Equally, the style of conflicts: formal battlefields, garrison duty, guerrilla and irregular warfare, and even maritime service, all required adaptation in uniforms, equipment and weapons. By 1660, the English soldier had all but fully evolved into the legendary redcoat. While Charles II formally disbanded the Protectorate army that had carved out this island's first global role he immediately commenced re-raising the Crown's own standing army from the veterans of the old.

Opposite.

This pikeman of the recreated Fairfax battalia is equipped in full armour. English Heritage.

Chronology

1639

The First Bishops' War. King's attempt to invade Scotland collapses and peace concluded by Pacification of Berwick (June).

1640

Second Bishops' War. Covenanter army under Alexander Leslie wins Battle of Newburn (28 August) and captures Newcastle thus forcing King to accept humiliating Treaty of Ripon (14 October).

1641

Outbreak of Rebellion in Ireland (October). Leads to raising of an English army intended for its re-conquest.

1642

First English regiments arrive in Ireland (February). King raises his standard at Nottingham Castle (22 August). After initial skirmish at Powick Bridge (23 September), the Earl of Essex is defeated by the King at the Battle of Edgehill (23 October). After making Oxford his capital, the King advances on London. Although Brentford is successfully stormed (12 November), the King is checked at Turnham Green by the London Trained Bands and Essex's army (13 November) and both sides retire to winter quarters.

1643

Essex captures Reading (27 April). The Northern Royalists under the Earl of Newcastle comprehensively defeats Lord Fairfax at the Battle of Adwalton Moor (30 June) securing their hold on much of the North, although Hull still holds out. The Western Royalists under Sir Ralph Hopton gain the upper hand with Sir William Waller's army destroyed at the Battle of Roundway Down (13 July) and Prince Rupert storming Bristol (26 July). The King lays siege to Gloucester (10 August), which Essex successfully relieves (8 September). The King intercepts Essex at

the Battle of Newbury (20 September), but after a fierce fight is obliged to draw off leaving the road to Reading and London open for Essex.

1644

The Scots Army under Lord Leven crosses the border (19 January), tipping the balance in favour of the Parliamentarians. English troops from Ireland are landed to re-enforce Lord Byron's Royalist forces in Cheshire but are almost totally destroyed at the Battle of Nantwich (25 January). Sir William Waller defeats the Royalists under Lord Forth and Hopton at the Battle of Cheriton (29 March) thereby halting their advance on London. Waller is subsequently defeated by the King at Cropredy Bridge (29 June). Rupert defeats Sir John Meldrum at the Battle of Newark, successfully relieving town (21 March). Marching from Shrewsbury, Rupert storms through Lancashire seizing Stockport (25 May), Bolton (28 May) and Liverpool (10 June). Having relieved siege of York (1 July), Rupert and the Earl of Newcastle are defeated by the combined armies of Leven, the Earl of Manchester and Lord Fairfax at the Battle of Marston Moor (2 July). Consequently the Royalists lose control of the North. The King surrounds Essex's Army in Cornwall and compels all but the horse to surrender near Fowey after the Battle of Lostwithiel (2 September). James, Marquess of Montrose leads Scottish Royalists to victory over the Covenanter's at the Battle of Tippermuir (1 September). Whilst relieving Royalist garrisons at Basing and Donnington Castle, Parliament successfully concentrates forces double that of the King's army and obliges him to fight the Second Battle of Newbury (27 October). Despite their numerical advantage they fail to crush the king.

1645

Recriminations among Parliamentary leaders brings about the formation of the New Model Army (NMA) under the determined leadership of Sir Thomas Fairfax (February-April). The NMA defeats the King's

Opposite.

Well equipped musketeers of the recreated Fairfax Battalia.

English Heritage.

'Oxford' Army at the Battle of Naseby (14 June), capturing most of its veteran infantry and guns. The NMA then defeats the Western Royalists under Lord Goring at the Battle of Langport (10 July). Rupert is obliged to surrender Bristol (10 September) thus forcing a Royalist retreat in the West back into Devon. The King, attempting to relieve Chester is defeated at the Battle of Rowton Heath (24 September). The King retires to Oxford. In Scotland, Montrose defeats a Covenanter army at the Battle of Kilsyth (15 August), forcing the Scottish army in England to abandon siege of Hereford and march north. David Leslie decisively defeats Montrose's under strength forces at Battle of Philiphaugh (13 September).

1646

The NMA drives ruthlessly west, ultimately defeating Hopton's army at the Battle of Torrington (16 February). The last Royalist field army, under Lord Astley, is compelled to surrender after a sharp action at Stow-on-the-Wold (21 March). The King surrenders to the Scots outside of Newark (5 May). Oxford surrenders (24 June).

1647

Welsh Royalists defiantly hold out in Harlech Castle until 15 March. Thereafter the Royalists have no strongholds on the mainland, although isolated Royalists forces hold out in the Isle of Man, the Channel Islands and the Isles of Scilly.

1648

The Second Civil War. Rowland Laugharne and John Poyer revolt in Wales (March) but Laugharne defeated at the Battle of St.Fagans (8 May). Oliver Cromwell besieges and re-takes Poyer in Pembroke Castle (11 July). Cromwell then marches North and comprehensively defeats Hamilton and the Northern Royalists at the Battle of Preston (17 August). Meanwhile, Fairfax defeats the Royalists of Kent at Battle of Maidstone (1 June) and then crosses Thames to counter Royalists in Essex, besieging Colchester (12 June to 28 August). Royalist garrison of Pontefract Castle holds out until 22 March 1649.

1649

Cromwell, Ireton and the Independents contrive the trial of King Charles, who is beheaded (30 January).

1649-50

Parliament's commander in Ireland, Michael Jones, inflicts decisive defeat on Irish Royalists under Earls of Ormonde and Inchiquin at Battle of Rathmines (2 August). Cromwell subsequently arrives and bloodily stormed Drogheda (11 September) and Wexford (11 October) thus crushing organised resistance.

1650

Cromwell returns to England to lead army against the Scots, leaving Henry Ireton to continue war against continuing Irish resistance. Cromwell defeats David Leslie at the Battle of Dunbar (3 September).

1651

English troops under John Lambert and John Okey rout Scottish army under Leslie at Battle of Inverkeithing (20 July). Scottish army under Leslie, the Duke of Hamilton and Charles II marches into England (August). Cromwell defeats them at the Battle of Worcester (3 September).

1652-54

The First Anglo-Dutch war, entirely fought at sea. The Commonwealth Navy secures a decisive victory at sea establishing England as a major maritime power. Glencairn's Royalist uprising in Scottish Highlands suppressed (1653-54).

1655

A small Royalist rising by Colonel John Penruddock in Wiltshire is quickly crushed (March). England subjected to systematic military rule of the Major-Generals. Anglo-Spanish War commences. Dispatch of an English army to conquer Spanish colony of Hispaniola in the Caribbean. Defeated outside City of San Domingo (April-May). Subsequently successful in conquest of Jamaica (May).

1657

After conclusion of Anglo-French treaty, dispatch of English troops to Flanders to carry fight to the Spanish Lowlands.

1658

Victory at the Battle of the Dunes (4 June). English garrison established in Dunkirk.

Death of the Lord Protector, Oliver Cromwell, who is succeeded by his ineffective son, Richard (3 September).

1659

Sir George Booth's rising in Cheshire, Lancashire and North Wales is crushed by Lambert at action of Winnington Bridge (19 August).

1660

Having crossed the border at Coldstream (1 January), George Monck ultimately brings about Restoration of Charles II with troops from his garrison in Scotland (29 May).

Opposite.

This recreated harquebusier is extremely well equipped, with a buff-coat, three bar pot, back and breast and full length boots.
English Heritage.

The Military Revolution 1600-1642

It is impossible to appreciate the arming, equipping and clothing of a mid-seventeenth century soldier without an appreciation of the broader military context within which the various conflicts occurred. In raising the various armies that fought across Britain and Ireland during the 1640s and 50s, the officers operated within the conceptual parameters already established by several decades of conflict, both in the Lowlands between the Dutch and Spanish, and more recently in Germany by the Swedes and other combatants of the Thirty Years War.

The Dutch Revolution in Warfare

Few would argue that the Dutch military systems developed by Prince Maurice and his cousins in Holland's long war with Spain were anything but revolutionary. While the tactics and drill of their Spanish opponents had been evolving through practical experiment and the on going modification of existing systems, as is well analysed by the work of Dr. Geoffrey Parker, the turn of the century saw the Dutch move to a military system of unique distinction. As so often with such leaps in military science, Prince Maurice did not so much invent as combine existing practice and ideas into a new and successful military system.

Prince Maurice's revolution can be traced back to the work of the Dutch scholar, Justus Lipsius, who, as a professor of history at the University of Leiden from 1579 to 1590 wrote *De Militia Romana*, published 1595, which recounted and analysed the various Roman and Greek military writers such as Aelian, Vegetius and Leo. Whilst these classical sources had never been forgotten, Lipsius's work brought them back into the spotlight where the young Prince Maurice of Nassau read it. Maurice, using the Roman military text-book of Vegetius, created the modern language of the drill-ground and command. The spread of Maurice's system was assisted in 1607 with the publication of Jacob de Gheyn's highly influential illustrated manual of arms handling, the *Wapenhandlingen van roers, musquetten ende spiessen*. While limited to the simple loading drill for the caliver and musket along with the handling of the pike, it none the less offered a very straightforward visual introduction to the rest of the new Dutch system. The popularity of this manual is revealed by its rapid translation into French, English, German and Danish. The *Wapenhandlingen* had been sponsored by John II of Nassau, Maurice's cousin and John further assisted in the spread of his cousin's military system, while also making some money from the enterprise, by establishing at Siegen in late 1616 the Kriegs and Ritteschule, one of the first modern schools for studying the art of war. While, by the time it closed in 1623, only some twenty students had attended, the school's first director, Johann Jacobi von Wallhausen, a professional German soldier, had been spurred on to write several comprehensive military manuals for cavalry and foot, *Kriegskunst zu Fuss* (1615), *Manuale Militare, Oder Krieggs Manual* (1616), *Archiley Kriegskunst* (1617), *Kunstliche Picquen-Handlung* (1617), *Defensio Patriar oder Landrettung* and *Kriegs-Kunst zu Pferd* (1617). Rapidly translated into French, these works were liberally plundered by English and other foreign authors over the next fifty years such as John Cruso's 1632 *Militarie Instructions for the Cavallerie*, which many horsemen of the English Civil War based their practice upon. In this manner the Dutch system was further entrenched in military literature as the common European model.

The basic concept of Maurice's military system was the combination of the tactical advantages of musketry firepower, pioneered in Italy by the Spanish Army in its Spanish, Italian and German tercios; and the greater scope offered by smaller, mutually

supporting units copied from the example of the classical Roman Army. This produced a quite different tactical structure with units in smaller, shallower formations drawn up in successive battle lines which would become the familiar pattern of warfare over the next two hundred years. The new tactical units became known as 'Battalions' which were drawn up ten ranks deep rather than the forty or more of the Spanish tercios. The tactical formation they fought in though saw the most fundamental change: the massive blocks of troops used by the Spanish, often up to 8,000 men, were replaced by the far more flexible system of triple battle lines copied from the ancient Roman *Triplex Acies*. This Dutch military system, with its mix of evolutionary and revolutionary military theory, went on to influence the developing military trends in Northern Germany which Gustavus Adolphus drew upon for his own inspiration and later military reforms

and these helped complete the revolution in firepower.

The young Gustavus Adolphus had been introduced by his Dutch tutor, Johan Skytte, to both Roman military literature and the developing Dutch military innovations. In 1608 he had received two months of intensive training from the Dutch veteran Jakob de la Gardie in Maurice's new system. The young King even visited Maurice's cousin, John II of Nassau in May 1620 where he discussed military issues and recent developments. Consequently, the entire foundation of Sweden's military system was Dutch, as can be seen in the detail of the individual training of officers and men, by the infantry's organisation into 550 man battalions, the adoption of linear tactics, and particularly its drill manual. The *Kriegs Kunst nach Koniglicher Schwedischer Manier* (Art of War in the Royal Swedish Manner) which was first printed in 1638, was the Swedish army's first detailed drill manual, yet most of it was a simple re-working of Wallhausen's 1615 drill manual *Kriegskurst zu Fuss* with the illustrations re-drawn to reflect 1630s clothing fashion. Gustavus did not in any sense alter the essentials of this system, rather he perfected it based on his own military experience in Poland and Germany from 1614. His key innovative idea was a new formation, the 'Swedish Brigade', a complex

This pikeman, again taken from de Gheyn, reflects the ideal around the turn of the century. By 1640 the use of armour by the pike was in sharp decline. PEW.

formation of four (later three) mutually supporting 'squadrons' (this was modelled on the Dutch battalion or half-regiment) of pike and shot which was effective for both the defense and offence. Gustavus's key tactical objective was the combination of mobility, firepower and the offensive. To this end he reduced the standard depth of infantry formations from Maurice's ten deep files down to six, and for maximum fire effect developed the delivery of fire by doubling the six ranks into three and having them all fire in a single devastating 'salvee'. This massive blast of musketry was supported by the fire of specially developed light artillery pieces which Gustavus introduced, immediately followed by an assault designed to smash any enemy staggered by the shock of such concentrated firepower. The draw back for Gustavus' 'Swedish System' was that it required a high ratio of trained officers to ranks along with continuous training and complex levels of organisation. While the reduction of formations to six ranks and the use of the three rank salvee were to be generally adopted, few if any army, even the later Swedish Army, were to adopt his tactical formations, preferring to remain with the simpler linear Dutch ones.

Gustavus, as a consequence of his campaign experience against the aggressive Polish horse, equally trained his own cavalry to utilise the same principles of mobility and offensive action. Previously, the majority of West European horse relied on their pistols as their primary weapon, each rank riding up, firing and then retiring to reload by 'caracole'. Gustavus trained the Swedish horse to charge home at point of sword, reserving their pistols for any melee which followed. Until copied by his enemies, the Swedish horse literally smashed its stationary opponents. The power of this tactic was increased by yet another innovation, that of mixing detached bodies of shot with squadrons of horse to give direct fire support against enemy bodies of horse immediately prior to a charge. Needless to say, a certain Prince Rupert was to utilise, and in some respects perfect, both these tactics, almost single handedly bringing this aspect of Swedish innovation to the English battlefield given the otherwise predominance of the Dutch school.

For England, the mechanism for the transmission of this knowledge was very straight forward as since the 1560s a steady stream of young Englishmen had been serving in the various regiments of the Anglo-Dutch Brigade in the long war with Spain. Later, with the commencement of the Thirty Years War, this foreign service expanded to include Swedish and German armies, and hence a direct tap into the most advanced contemporary military concepts. The dominance of the Dutch school though was maintained throughout due to a national bias in favour of English service with the Dutch. The list of both Parliamentarian and Royalist officers who learned their trade in Dutch service is long, ranging from the Earl of Essex, Lord Astley and Prince Rupert, to many lesser known officers such as Gervase Hollis, Sir Stephen Hawkins and the Byron brothers. The list who served in allied German Protestant armies is shorter, including officers such as Lord Hopton, Sir William Waller and Sydenham Poyntz. Hardly any English officers of the Civil War appear to have served in the Swedish army, Sir Arthur Aston being a notable exception. Meanwhile, the majority of professional Scots officers were dominated by Swedish service, the Earl of Leven, David Leslie, Sir Alexander Hamilton, William Baillie, the Lumsden brothers, Lord Forth, Lord Eythin and the notable author, Sir James Turner. It was therefore not surprising that all English infantry manuals and hence armies were to be dominated by the Dutch military system.

For the bulk of officers though who were to

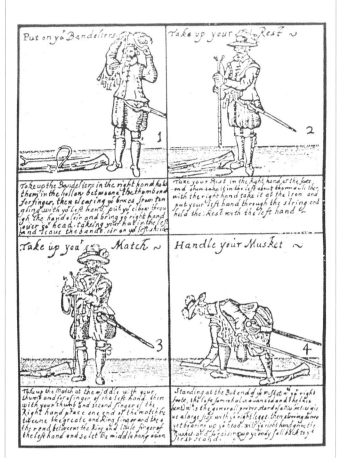

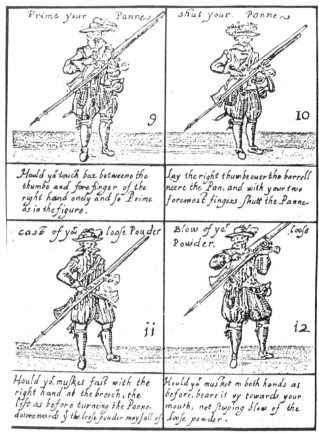

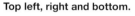

Top left, right and bottom.

In the fourteen years prior to the civil war the king took significant steps towards improving the county trained bands. This included the publication and distribution of drill manuals. These pages come from the manual 'Directions for Musters' (1638). Not only do they accurately reflect the style of clothing and equipment expected of the ordinary musketeer on the eve of conflict, this work was widely utilised by both sides in the war for training. PEW.

command troops in Britain's wars of the 1640s and 50s, it was the written works produced by a number of these veterans which proved vital. Invariably they were more than simple drill manuals as they also described in detail how infantry, cavalry and artillery should be equipped and clothed and in some works, how to go about organising this. The first of these was that of the English veteran of Dutch service, Captain John Bingham. His book *The Tactiks of Aelian Or art of embattailing an army after ye Grecian manner*, published in 1616, presented the English reader with their first comprehensive account of Maurice's military concepts and thinking, linking them to the ancient Greek and Roman texts. Most fundamentally, Bingham included as a seven page appendix to his book a copy of the basic Dutch drill manual as used by English troops in

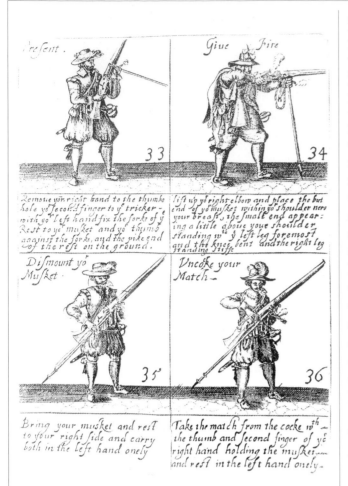

Present. 33

Remoue yonright hand to the thumbe hole ye second finger to y tricker with yo left hand fix the forke of y Rest to ye musket and yo thumb against the forke, and the pike end of the rest in the ground.

Giue Fire 34

lift up yo right elbow and place the but end of yo musket within yo shoulder nere your breast, the small end appearing a little aboue youe shoulder standing wth y left leg foremost and the knee bent and the right leg standing stiffe

Dismount yo Musket. 35

Bring your musket and rest to your right side and carry both in the left hand onely

Uncoke your Match. 36

Take the match from the cocke wth the thumb and second finger of yo right hand holding the musket and rest in the left hand onely.

Musket drill. See caption on previous page. PEW

Dutch service *The Exercise of the English in the service of the high and mighty Lords, the Lords of the Estates of the United Provinces in the Low Countries.* This manual was to became the primary source for many subsequent English language works on infantry drill and equipment, especially the official militia instructions of 1623 and 1638. As part of a drive to improve the basic quality of the English trained bands, in 1623 *Instructions For Musters and Armes, And the use therof: By order from the Lords of His maiesties most Honourable Privy Counsayle* was distributed, followed in 1638 by *Directions for Musters.* These were then heavily drawn upon in 1641 for the generally available *The Exercise of the English in the Militia of the Kingdome of England.* Subsequently, the King's regulations for his Oxford based army published in late 1642 and early 1643 included a military drill manual which was almost a verbatim copy of the 1638 *Directions.*

Another key source making available to the English reader later Dutch practice was the work of Henry Hexham. While Hexham was never to serve in any English army or in the English Civil War, he had a major impact upon both in terms of the transmission of the most up to date Dutch systems. Hexham had commenced his military career in 1601 as a page to Sir Francis Vere at the Siege of Ostend. He continued in Dutch service in its English Regiments, holding the rank of Captain-Quartermaster, first in 1629 in Lord Horace Vere's Regiment and then from 1636 in the Hon. George Goring's Regiment. While Hexham did, periodically, return to England, he demonstrated no desire to serve in English service, receiving a pass to return to Holland in July 1640 at the height of the mobilisation for the Second Bishops' War. 'Captain-Quartermaster Henry Hexham' was still listed on the strength of Colonel 'Killegreuw's' Regiment in 1649, and as late as 15th May 1651, the memorials of Gervase Holles records a letter from 'Olde Captain Hexham' from Holland on the topic of one of Gervase's relatives in Dutch service, 'Leiuetenant Colonell Thomas Holles'. This veteran of Dutch service was also a prolific writer, producing various accounts of military actions he had participated in, an exhaustive military manual and even English language editions of Dutch atlases and a dictionary. The British Library lists fifteen works by him.

Hexham's first works which appeared in English were his accounts of various sieges, *A historicall Relation of the…Siege of the Busse, and the surprising of Wesell,* (1630), *A Journal of the taking of Venlo, Raermont, Strale, the memorable Siege of Mastricht, the Towne & Castle of Limburch uner…the Prince of Orange,* (1633), *A true and brief relation of the famous siege of Breda: besieged and taken in under the able and victorious conduct of His Highness the Prince of Orange,* (1637) and an English translation of Marolois's The Art of Fortification (1638). These offered the English reader an account of the most recent Dutch developments in this key military art as well as providing a reminder of the participation of English Protestant volunteers in the continuing war against Catholic Spain. It was his military manual though, *The Principles of the Art Militaire; practised in the Warres of the United Netherlands,* first published in London in 1637 and subsequently updated in its 1642 second edition, that had most impact. Its first fifty pages included a definition of each rank's duties, a comprehensive set of illustrations showing the musket and pike handling movements and a set of fine engravings demonstrating how to drill and manoeuvre an infantry company. The remaining parts of the work dealt with various military subjects such as the laying out of a military camp, how to conduct sieges, the order of an army on the march and so on. In 1642 a second edition was published which, while largely a re-print of the 1637 edition, did include additional diagrams of battle orders and manoeuvres that had occurred between these dates.

That these English veterans of Dutch service were drawn upon by English military writers who had never seen active military service can be demonstrated by the many references to them in their own works. For example, in William Barriffe's *Militarie Discipline: or The Young Artillery-man*, possibly one of the most read manuals before and after the English Civil War given it ran to six editions between 1635 and 1661, he states in reference to performing ranks, files and dignities: 'I might here demonstrate unto you the several opinions of Leo, Robertellus, Count Mansfield, Sir Tho. Kellie, and many others: but their works being extant, I will spare the labour. Nevertheless I will say thus much, that Cap. John Bingham, although somewhat obscurely, yet in my judgement hath best delivered himself concerning this particular'.

A number of the key English military authors in the seven years prior to the Civil War, while they had seen no active military service, were crucially linked by the various voluntary military 'Societies' operating in London to veterans of the Dutch service and to each other. The second decade of the seventeenth century had seen a marked increase in enthusiasm for military matters in England and particularly in London. This had resulted in not only a general revival of the militia but also, commencing with the 'Society of the Artillery Garden' and soon followed by the 'Military Company of Westminster' and the 'Martial Yard' in Southwark, a revitalisation of the voluntary groups.

Made up of the wealthier London citizens, the history of these voluntary groups dated back to Tudor times. The two key locations were the New Artillery Yard in Bishopsgate and the Military Garden in St.Martin's Fields. Gunnery had been practised in the Old Artillery Yard (very close to the 'New') as far back as 1537 when it was leased by the gunners of the Tower. By 1585 the Guild of St.George, better known as the Honourable Artillery Company, were specifically using the New Artillery Yard for training. The skill of these volunteers was recognised when several were appointed to command troops at Tilbury in 1588 and they became known as the 'Captains of the Artillery Yard'.

While the 1590s and the first decade of the seventeenth century had seen enthusiasm for military matters decline, this period came to an end with the opening stages of the Thirty Years War and by 1620 the members were meeting regularly to practice arms drill and manoeuvre, the intricacies of which now became seen as a social accomplishment. These groups often hired veterans of the Dutch service to tutor them in Maurice's military system. The first was no less a person than Captain John Bingham, who was

The liner under this recreated pikeman's helmet is just visible.
English Heritage.

appointed in the early 1620s to train the Honourable Artillery Company. In 1629, Bingham wrote a second part to his 1616 classic *The Art of Embattailing an Army, or The Second Part of Aelians Tacticks*. It was specifically dedicated to the: 'President of the martiall Company, Exercising Armes in the Artillery garden in London. To Captaine Henry Waller, Now Captaine of the Said company and To all the Rest of the Worthy Captaines and Gentlemen of the said Company'. (Barriffe, writing his manual only a few years later specifically details 'Captain Wallers triple firing to the Front').

A second such respected veteran of Dutch service, Philip Skippon, was appointed in October 1639 as 'Captain-Leader' to the Society of the Artillery Garden. Skippon, while he did not himself produce any manuals, was undoubtedly a dynamic source for the dominance of the Dutch model being well versed in the technical writings of the period. Shortly after his first taste of action, Skippon entered service under Sir Horace Vere in the Palatinate in 1620. He subsequently spent over fifteen years serving in the Anglo-Dutch Brigades alongside the likes of the Earl of Essex, Sir Thomas Fairfax, George Monke, Sir Ralph Hopton, Sir Richard Grenville, Lord George Goring and many others who would rise to prominence in the Civil War. Returning to England in 1638 to take over the small family estate left by his father, he soon tired of the farming life and accepted employment in the Artillery Garden. A close friend of Skippon's was John Cruso dating back to his service in the Dutch army. It was Cruso who wrote in 1632 the influential *Militarie Instructions for the Cavall'rie*, and Skippon was almost certainly the close friend to whom Cruso dedicated: 'The one (during the short discontinuance from his regiment, while it lay in winter garrison) hath been courteously pleased to go through it, correcting what here and there was amisse, suplying some things defective, and manifesting his approbation of it with an Imprimatur'.

Skippon also encouraged Cruso to translate the Sieur du Praissac's military manual *The Art of Warre, or Militarie discourses* which was published in England in 1639, and Skippon's own military library contained one of the only two manuscript copies of Sir Francis Vere's *Commentaries* used by William Dillingham for his printed edition in 1657. It was this key mix of practical experience and technical knowledge that caused the Society of the Artillery Garden to appoint him their 'Captain-Leader' in October 1639. A third such appointee was Henry Tillier who had been Captain-Leader of the Military Company of Westminster in the 1630s.

Reflecting their teaching, a leading member of the Artillery Garden then went on to write the most detailed of the pre-war manuals, William Barriffe's *The Young Artillery-man* in 1635 which he dedicated to all the officers of the London Trained bands and, in a slightly later edition, specifically to 'Philip Skippon'. Robert Ward, while he was not a member but was closely associated with this group, wrote the major military study of the art of war, *Anima'Adversions of Warre* in 1639. After the Civil War an officer of the Military Company of Westminster, Richard Elton, wrote the major post war military manual, *The Compleat Body of the Art Military* in 1650 where he made clear both the reliance on Continental experience and his specific debt to Henry Tillier: 'and farther, to my best remembrance, I never could meet with any souldier that hath been abroad upon any service that ever saw any charging of the Pikes at the Foot,...In my opinion the best way of opposing the Horse charge is that which we learned of our ever honoured Captain, Major Henry Tillier, in the Military Garden'.

Further, not only did members of these voluntary societies traditionally provide officers of the London Trained Bands which made up such a key part of Parliament's forces in the Civil War, many, especially the authors, went on to become senior officers in regular regiments. Barriffe became Sergeant-Major in Colonel John Hampden's Regiment of Foot, while Elton went on to become Sergeant-Major in the City of London Auxiliaries. Of the tutors, two went on to become generals in their own rights, Skippon for Parliament and Tillier for the King. After the war, as an example of professionalism overcoming political bias, the Parliamentarian Richard Elton praised, as was noted above, his ex-tutor, the Royalist General Henry Tillier.

This method of transmission would not have had such an impact if it had not been for the almost institutionalised tradition of foreign service. Commencing with the dispatch of the first volunteers to join the Dutch in their struggle with Spain in 1572, English soldiers in Dutch service became a permanent institution until almost the end of the seventeenth century. While varying in size, the Anglo-Dutch Brigade saw thousands of young English Protestants serving in the long struggle in the Low Countries and, as has already been indicated, conveying this experience and knowledge back to England. A single but fundamental example of this process was illustrated by the network that was built up at the commencement of the seventeenth century which linked the Vere family, the Holles family and Henry Hexham.

For almost forty years spanning the end of the sixteenth century and the beginning of the seventeenth, two cousins of the Earl of Oxford, Sir Francis Vere and then Sir Horace Vere commanded first the Anglo-Dutch Brigade in Dutch service and then the English force sent to assist Frederick and Elizabeth in the Palatinate in 1620. The many thousands of young English Protestants who served under them mostly fell into two broad classes; firstly those who participated for a brief time, a campaign or two, seeing it as much as part of their overall education, and secondly those who saw it as a career and expected to remain in Dutch service for a considerable amount of time. Many well known soldiers of the Civil Wars fell into the first group, the Earl of Essex and Sir Thomas Fairfax being two such. The second and smaller group included many of the leading officers of the Civil War such as Sir Philip Skippon, Lord Astley, George Goring, Robert Berty the First Earl of Lindsey and his son Lord Willoughby, Lord Charles Gerard, Charles Lucas, Francis Mackworth and George Monck. That these

These recreated pikeman, whilst still armoured have dispensed with the tassets. English Heritage.

officers did identify themselves as professional career officers can be inferred by the significant number, providing they were still in good health, who, at the end of the Civil War in 1646, returned to foreign service, albeit in the French and Spanish army as well as the Dutch (an indication of the universality of the Dutch military system). There was though a small third group where, as with the Vere brothers, it became almost a family tradition to take up such service and where some members even transferred their English families to the Low Countries or married Dutch wives. Various members of the Holles family well illustrate all three categories.

The mid-seventeenth century antiquarian, Gervase Holles, himself a Royalist Colonel during the Civil War, produced an extensive history of his family. Gervase recorded in his 'Memorials of the Holles Family' how one of his great cousins, Edward Holles, 'In his youth he had beene a souldier and trayled a pike for some years in the Netherlands' during the latter half of Elizabeth's reign before returning to England to marry and raise a family. Another great cousin, Sir George Holles, personified the

professional English soldier: 'he was sent to the University of Cambridge by John Holles, his elder brother, from whence after some time of continuance he made a sally (his genius inclining more to the active trade of a souldier than to the sedentary life of a scholar) into the Netherlands where he trayl'd a pike some years in the company of his famous kinsman, Sir Francis Vere. Being enter'd into the profession under so great a maister of it he gave over his thoughtes of England and resolved to set up his rest in the Low Country in that calling wch best suited with the greatness and activity of his spirit; wherein indeed he became a principall honour both to his name and nation'.

Although he spent his entire life in Dutch service, rising to become a Colonel before his death on 13th May 1626, this highly respected soldier in the struggle against Catholic Spain was brought back to England to be buried alongside Sir Francis Vere whose cousin he was and under whose command he mostly served.

During his long service, Sir George Holles served alongside Henry Hexham, who in 1623, dedicated his first published piece of writing to him. Of George's two brothers, the youngest, Thomas, also took up a military career becoming a Lieutenant-Colonel in the

Sir Thomas Lunsford's Foot, October 1642.

At the commencement of the war the soldiers of both sides, but particularly the Royalists, mostly still wore their civilian clothes and were grateful for a few military items seized from the arsenals of the trained bands or from stores originally destined for Ireland. In the plate opposite, an officer and a sergeant of Sir Thomas Lunsford's Foot are inspecting the best equipped of their pike and shot having 'fetch'd from thence [Wincanton] a magazeene of armes that had been deposited there a yeare or two before…'. As with their comrades in the background, the two soldiers still wear the rather drab civilian clothes common to agricultural workers, as are the pikeman's footwear of calf-length startups. Equally originating from a common item of civilian attire, the musketeer and many of the pikemen in the background wear a knitted, woollen Monmouth cap, the musketeers having a brim to mimic the appearance of the gentry's fashionable broad brimmed hats. As with many Royalist shot, the musketeer has a powder bag on his right manufactured from 'Calfe skinns tanned and oyled', sharing a 'girdle' with a pattern sword. The pikeman is astonishingly well equipped compared to the majority of his colleagues, having an iron pot, corselet and tassets along with a pattern sword. However, as the war progressed, apart from iron pots, the use of body armour declined thus making the body of pike being drilled by their corporal and using just sixteen foot pikes more representative. In the absence of any other distinguishing items, both musketeer and pikeman wear coloured ribbons tied around their upper right arms to identify their company.

The sergeant is identifiable by his halbert and red sash, the common badges of his rank. His good quality red suit suggests he is a professional soldier, red already being established as a military colour. Whilst not heavily laced, he is nonetheless clothed as a gentleman, with a felt hat, good quality sword and bucket topped boots. Observing from behind the sergeant, is a gentleman and officer. Apart from the richness of his apparel and appointments, with a fine suit of doublet and breeches, a laced linen shirt and bucket topped boots, his rank is clearly indicated by the black and gold gorget worn around his neck. Painting by Christa Hook.

Dutch army and marrying a Dutch nobleman's daughter. His family grew up in Holland where he died and was buried. Even George's elder brother John served for a few years in the Low Countries before returning to become the Earl of Clare.

Of Gervase's own branch of the family, his grandfather, Sir Gervase Holles briefly served as a volunteer in the Anglo-Dutch Brigade before returning home to marry and inherit the estate. Both his sons, Francis and Frescheville served in the Low Countries, Captain Francis Holles later becoming Muster Master of Nottinghamshire's Militia. The author of this family history, Gervase, was the only son of Frescheville and was hence not allowed, as he wanted, to see active service, instead he was sent to the Middle Temple to become a lawyer. Yet his opportunity came in 1642 when he became first a Captain, then a Major and finally a Colonel, in the Royalist army. Gervase's first command was as a Captain in Sir Lewis Dyve's Regiment of Foot where his cousin, William Holles, one of the son of Captain Francis Holles, became a Lieutenant. Later, the by then Captain William Holles was to die at Newark in March 1644. In exile during the 1650s in the Low Countries, Gervase met 'olde Capt. Hexham' who passed on considerable details of Gervase's various relations' military service. The extensive account reads like a who's who of English officers of the Anglo-Dutch Brigade.

Yet it was not only through this extensive network of family links that Sir George Holles played his part in transferring the Dutch military system to England, for in 1625: 'his Matie finding it requisite to have the trayned bandes of England more strictly disciplin'd and fitted (upon any occasion) for a posture of war, sent over a command to Sir George Holles to select so many able and experienced souldiers as might be distributed (two into every county of England and Wales) for the better trayning and disciplining of the respective troupes and companies'.

The following January, Sir George arrived with 117 serjeants at St. Katherine's, Westminster from whence they were appointed as Muster Masters to every county militia in England. Only two years before, in 1623, *Instructions for Musters* had been produced as a key element in the attempt to improve England's county militia and transform it into an 'Exact Militia'. This work had been prefaced on Bingham's account of the Dutch military system. Sir George's 117 sergeants, fresh from the Low Countries, were to ensure its accurate implementation. It is interesting to note that this exercise was attempted a second time after the very poor showing of the English army during the First Bishop's War when Sir Nicholas Byron was ordered by the Council of War to find 100 expert soldiers and corporals from the Continent.

Equipment and Arms

Although the conflict raging across Europe during the 1620s and 1630s transferred revolutionary new concepts of drill, tactics and military formations, clothing and equipment developments were more evolutionary. Whilst qualitatively different from the troops who had fought in the late Tudor period, the style and standards of clothes and equipment expected of English soldiers in 1639 still reflected certain obsolete concepts and practices. These rapidly evaporated in the white heat of battle.

The Infantry

The majority of any army was the the infantry, composed of the standard shot and pike. Following the Dutch model, ideally a standard infantry regiment ought to have totalled between 1,000 and 1,200 men plus officers divided into10 companies for organisational purposes. Having said this there were exceptions, the personal regiments of army commanders often being larger. The Lord Lieutenant's regiment dispatched to Ireland in 1641 and the Earl of Essex's own Lord General's regiment in 1642 both numbered 1,500 men. Equally, the regiments of the London Trained Bands sometimes reached strengths of around 2,000 men. For regiments of 1,000 men, companies were of an equal size of 100 men each, this being generally the model followed in Scotland. More commonly in England, regiments were prefaced on 1,200 men divided into companies of varying size. These ranged from the colonel's company at 200 men, lieutenant-colonel's 160, major's 140 and the seven captain's companies 100 each. These totals only referred to the privates, the officers, both commissioned and non-commissioned, plus the drummers being separately counted. The numbers of commissioned officers was fairly standard at 33, regardless of whether companies were of an equal or unequal size, whereas the numbers of non-commissioned officers did vary slightly. Taking one of the Earl of Essex's regiments of 1642 as a model, the regimental staff included the colonel, lieutenant-colonel and sergeant-major, along with a number of specialists, who while not commissioned were more than simple non-commissioned officers (essentially embryonic warrant officers) including a Quartermaster, Provost Marshall, Chirurgeon (surgeon), Preacher, Waggon-Master, Drum Major and two Chirurgeon's Mates. For the ten companies, the colonel, lieutenant-colonel and major also acted as captains of the senior three, with substantive captains heading the remainder. Each company then had a lieutenant (a captain-lieutenant in the colonels company) and an ensign. In respect of the non-commissioned officers (including drummers who ranked as corporals), there were either 70 or 71. Whilst they did not hold a commission from the King, they were normally listed as 'officers' due to their position in the company. In the standard company of 100 men there were 2 sergeants, 3 corporals and 2 drummers. This was constant in all but the larger 200 strong colonel's company model, where this increased by 1 with an additional sergeant. In some regiments, but far from all, companies had 3 further 'officers', namely a 'gentleman-at-armes', a clerk and a 'lanspassadoe'. The former was responsible for inspecting the company's arms and the storage of its immediate supply of gunpowder, bullets and matchcord. Clerks sometimes appeared both on regimental staff and company strengths, their duty being to respectively keep the regimental or company muster rolls and to receive and distribute, under the captain's direction, the soldiers' pay. The lanspassadoe ranked below a corporal and had the duty to assist him. Whilst commonly mentioned in military manuals before the Civil War, they only appeared on the muster rolls of regiments of the Eastern Association.

Generally on the battlefield the prime tactical formation was the regiment. If a regiment was within a few hundred men of its established strength of 1,000 to 1,200, it was divided into three or four 'Grand

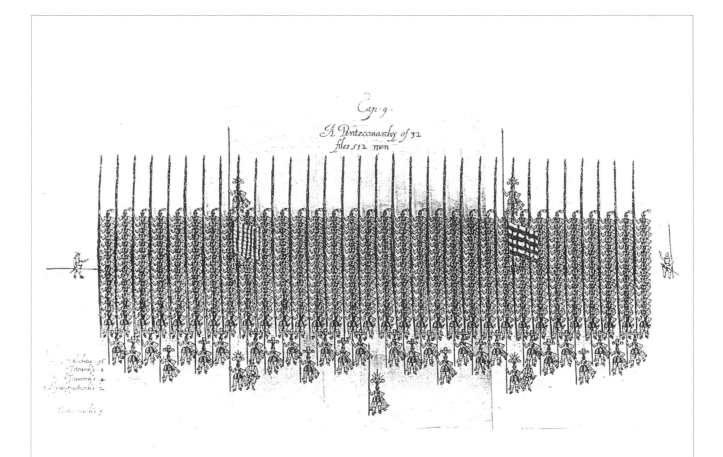

Top.
Drawn up in a series of divisions, this grand division of pikeman as illustrated by John Bingham in *Tactiks of Aelian* (c.1616) would have been flanked on either side by twice their number of shot. PEW.

Right and bottom.
When called upon the pike would close to 'push of pike', again as illustrated by Bingham. PEW.

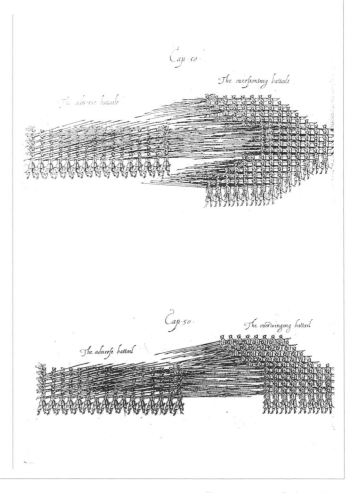

Divisons', each composed of two to three companies. Each Grand Division was drawn up with the pikemen formed as the central body flanked on either side by two equal wings of shot, all in files six to eight ranks deep. Each of these blocks of pike and shot was then sub-divided into equal divisions. In practice though, few regiments ever came close to the established totals, and regiments of 400 to 500 were the norm on campaign, normally dividing into just two Grand Divisions. Whilst Clarenden recorded that Sir Thomas Salisbury's regiment at Edgehill numbered 'twelve hundred poor Welsh vermin', such totals on the Royalist side were exceptional. While the regiments of senior figures such as Prince Rupert's Regiment of Foot and the King's Lifeguard managed to maintain totals of around 500 men apiece, more

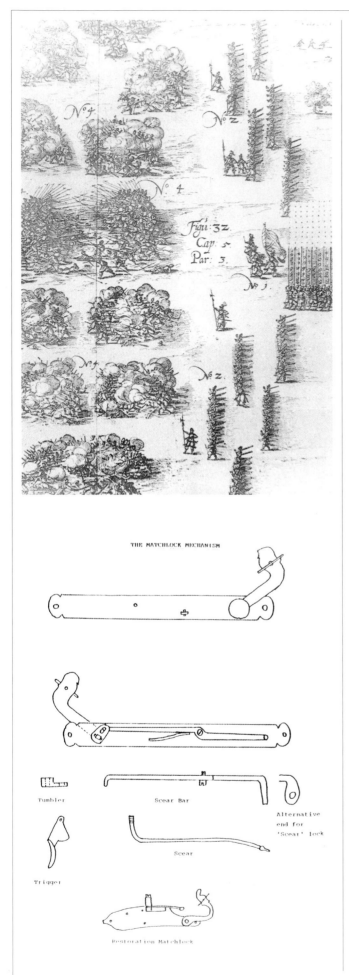

representative was the muster list taken at Reading in April 1644 of the King's Oxford Army. This not only revealed just how few men an average Royalist regiment fielded, but the very high ratio of officers to private soldiers, bearing in mind that the term officer included non-commissioned officers and drummers. Of the twelve regiments, the strongest was Sir William Pennyman's with 119 officers and 360 privates divided into 11 companies followed by Sir Charles Lloyd's (previously Salisbury's) with 101 officers and 308 privates in 10 companies. Although weaker in terms of privates to the latter of these, Sir Theophilus Gilby's, with 107 officers to 268 privates in 11 companies and Sir Stephen Hawkins' with 104 officers to 171 privates in 9 companies demonstrated the preference for maintaining smaller companies to absorb the higher ratios of officers. The number of companies could only be reduced when there were fewer officers, as demonstrated by Sir George Lisle's with just 81 officers to 189 privates in 8 companies and Sir John Owen's with 39 officers to 106 privates in 4 companies. At the bottom end of the scale were two regiments with an almost 1:2 ratio of officers to privates, William Euer's with 32 officers to 59 privates in 3 companies and Sir Thomas Blackwell's with 30 officers to 56 men in 4 companies. The simple fact was that private soldiers evaporated at an alarming rate whilst the officer cadres did not. Thus, if the 90 companies fielded by these twelve regiments had had their full complement of officers, there would have been a total of some 1,002, where in fact the muster returned a respectable 923. As for private soldiers, the same ninety companies ought to have fielded around 9,000 men, instead of just the 2,231 recorded. By June 1645, so weak were some regiments, they were brigaded together to effectively form composite formations, the 500 strong 'Shrewsbury Foot' composed of the remnants of Henry Tillier's, Robert Broughton's, Henry Warren's, Richard Gibson's and Sir Fulk Hunks' regiments being a prime example.

Broadly, Parliament appears to have managed to maintain the strength of its field regiments at a higher level than those of the King due to vigorous conscription in the latter stages of the war and its possession of the more densely populated parts of the

THE MATCHLOCK MECHANISM

Tumbler

Scear Bar

Alternative end for 'Scear' lock

Trigger

Scear

Restoration Matchlock

The sturdy matchlock mechanism would remain the dominant firearm for the infantry throughout the early and mid seventeenth century. Partizan Press.

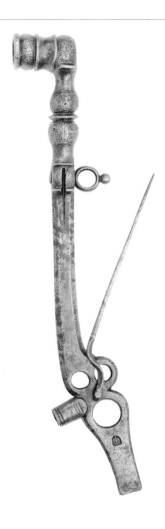

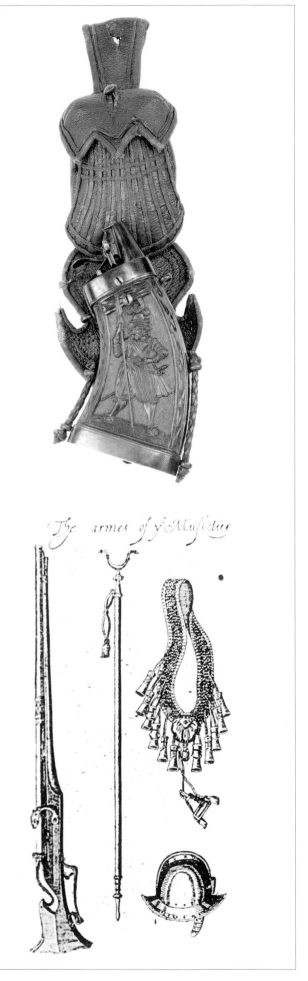

Top.
A combination tool for a wheel-lock gun, German (Nuremberg?) c.1600-1620, incorporating vent-pricker, screwdriver, two different sizes of spanner (for pistol and carbine?), and two dimensions of bullet-sizing hole (for pistol and carbine?). The Trustees of the Wallace Collection, A1320.

Top right.
A harquebusier's 'port-flask', powder horn and bullet-pouch, German (Saxon) c.1610. The Trustees of the Wallace Collection A1284.

Right.
Taken from Bingham's work of 1616, by the 1640s neither the musket rest or helmet played much part in musketeers equipment. PEW.

country, London, the south-east and East Anglia. At the commencement of campaigns, the regiments of senior officers and the London Trained Bands in fact often exceeded the standard totals. The Earl of Essex's in 1642 recorded 1,500 men whilst the Earl of Manchester's in May 1644 recorded 1,628. In September 1643 the Red Regiment of the London Trained Bands fielded a total of 2018 officers and men,

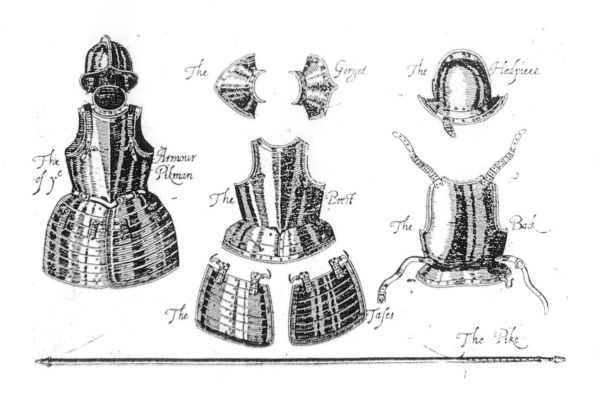

Also taken from Bingham, even in the early stages of the war few pikemen could aspire to such a complete set of armour. At best most made do with a back, breast, and helmet. PEW.

the Green Auxiliaries 1,200. More representative were the totals recorded for six of Essex's regiments in June 1644 as they entered the field against the King, the totals recorded being: Thomas Tyrell's 524, Lord Robarte's 700, Philip Skippon's 550, Richard Fortescue's 634, Henry Barclay's 475 and William Davies' 316. Equally, in the following month, four regiments of the Eastern Association of the Earl of Manchester's army outside of York recorded: Lawrence Crawford's 608, John Pickering's 524, Edward Montagu's 418 and Francis Russell's 662. Needless to say, apart from combat casualties, the impact of active campaigning in the wet and rainy weather of a century which was classified as a mini-ice age ensured heavy losses through sickness, exhaustion and simple desertion, soon whittling down even these respectable figures. By September 1644, of Montagu's six companies, whilst retaining full complements of officers, four had less than 30 men apiece and two just 11, and by January 1645 Pickering's had declined to 243 despite being in receipt of reinforcements. Equally, whilst Essex's regiments in June 1644

returned respectable numbers, in December 1643 their average strength had been barely 120 men.

The major impact of weak regiments with high officer cadres to both sides was two-fold: it ensured excessive costs and made it awkward to compose balanced formations on the battlefield. In an attempt to overcome these problems both sides during the winter of 1644/45 attempted to re-model their armies

Opposite.
Top left.
A fine English mortuary hilt sword c.1640. The Spence Collection, Sulgrave Manor.

Top right.
A close-up of the detail on the guard of the above. The Spence Collection, Sulgrave Manor.

Bottom left.
A swept hilted rapier with silver encrusted decoration, typical of Dutch and English taste of the first half of the seventeenth century. The Spence Collection, Sulgrave Manor.

Bottom right.
A German Pappenheimer style hilt. The Spence Collection, Sulgrave Manor.

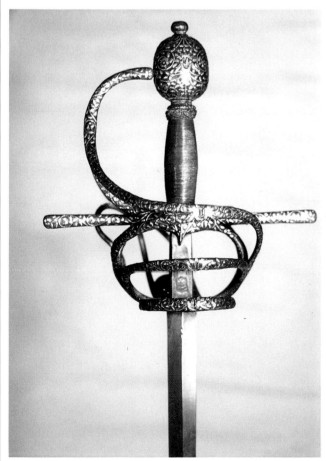

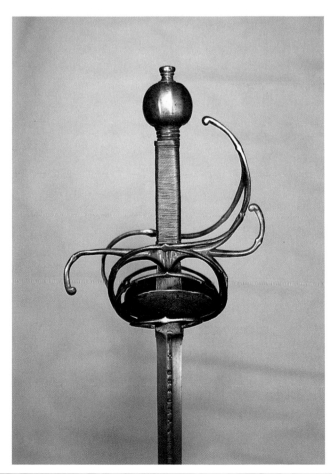

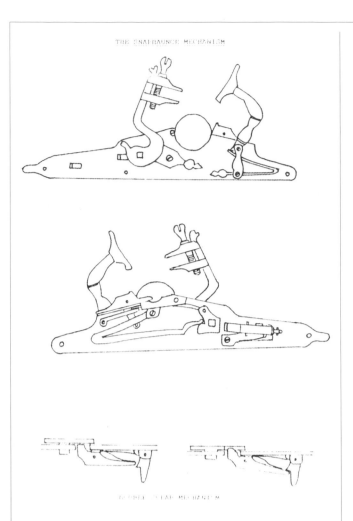

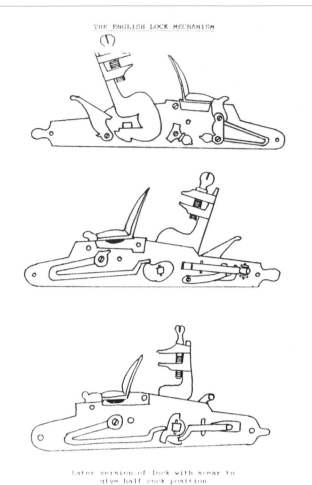

Top: left and right; opposite top: left and right.
In terms of new technology for the musketeer the new weapon
was the firelock. Although there were various styles of
mechanism in use during the civil war, the 'French lock'
ultimately came to be the dominant model and generically
referred to as the flintlock by late generations of soldiers.
Partizan Press.

by amalgamating weak regiments. Parliament
succeeded in the form of the New Model Army whilst
the King and Rupert failed, outmatched by the
entrenched vested interests of their supporters, an
outcome which played no small part in the King's
ultimate defeat. There was no little irony in
Parliament's formation of the New Model. Charles
and Rupert's essentially failed to break the essentially
feudal concept that each colonel had proprietorship of
their regiment. Conversely, one of the major reasons
Parliament had gone to war with the King was over
their concern at his absolutist centralising tendencies.
Yet they effectively dissolved the varied regiments of
the respective colonels, forcibly amalgamating them
and ensured all officers were directly appointed by
Parliament after satisfactory vetting. In achieving this,
Parliament went far beyond the centralising policies
tentatively pursued before the war. The New Model

was a modern standing army of the state, its funding,
equipping and the appointment of its officers being
Parliament's, to whom it owed allegiance.

On the battlefields of the Continent a number of
regiments were commonly brought together in
'tertias' or 'brigades'. This was a practice still finding
its way across the Channel as it does not appear to
have been adopted by Parliament. As late as Naseby,
the New Model Army deployed its infantry regiments
as individual formations and even later, at Preston in
1648, Dunbar 1650 and Worcester 1651, there was
still no evidence of organised brigades. This stood in
stark contrast to the armies under the King and
Rupert's direction who, from Edgehill onwards, were
generally organised prior to any battle into brigades/
tertias. Having said this, not all Royalist commanders
did so, Newcastle and Hopton being cases in point. As
for combat, much ink has been spilled over whether
formations fought in Swedish or Dutch order. In fact,
apart from the Royalists at Edgehill, the contemporary
Dutch formations and tactics, albeit modified by
Swedish innovations in respect of depth and method
of delivering firepower, were overwhelmingly predominant for all, including the Covenanters Scots and
Catholic Irish. Whilst the pike was considered by
military authors as the more honourable weapon in

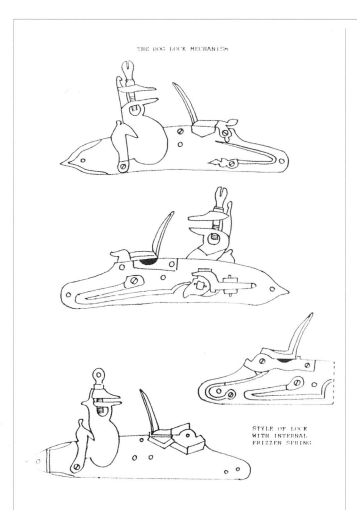

THE DOG LOCK MECHANISM

STYLE OF LOCK
WITH INTERNAL
FRIZZEN SPRING

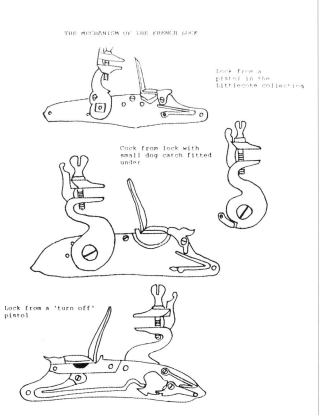

THE MECHANISM OF THE FRENCH LOCK

Lock from a
pistol in the
Littlecote collection

Cock from lock with
small dog catch fitted
under

Lock from a 'turn off'
pistol

comparison to the musket, its role was firmly subordinate during combat. It was essentially limited to protecting the shot from the opponent's horse and charging to push of pike once an opponent's formation had been sufficiently disrupted by the shot. The musketeers meanwhile delivered their fire increasingly by volley or 'salvee'. Whilst firing by rank was still utilised, each rank giving fire and then wheeling to the rear to allow the next successive rank to fire, this was generally only utilised at extended range. Rather, the divisions of shot would double up to just three ranks, give fire at close range in a single devastating salvee and then fall on with sword and butt-end of musket. Such a standard infantry assault from the Continent was described in two accounts from the Battle of Leipsig in 1631. Firstly, the Scots Brigade was recorded as: '...ordering themselves in several small battagliaes, about 6 or 700 in a body, presently now double their rankes, making their files then but 3 deepe, the discipline of the King of Sweden beeng neuer to march aboue 6 deepe. This done, the formost ranke falling on their knees; the second stooping forward; and the third ranke standing right up, and all giuing fire together; they powred so much lead at one instant in amongst the enemies horse that their ranckes were much broken with it'.

The second account was by an English officer who was second in command of Lumsden's regiment of Scots in the Brigade: 'First giving fire unto three little field-pieces that I had before me, I suffered not my musketeers to give their volleys, till I came within pistol-shot of the enemy; at which time I gave order to the three first rancks to discharge at once; and after them the other three: which done we fell pell mell into their rancks, knocking them down with the stock of the musket and our swords'.

Identical tactics were utilised in England, the above descriptions perfectly matching Sir Edward Walker's description of the Royalist assault at Naseby in 1645: 'Presently our forces advanced up the Hill, the Rebels only discharging Five Pieces at them, but over shot them, and so did their Musquetiers. The Foot on either side hardly saw each other until they were within Carabine Shot, and so made only one volley; ours falling in with Sword and butt end of the Musquet did notable execution, so much as I saw their Colours fall, and their Foot in great disorder...'.

At the turn of the century, the shot and pike had still been equipped to a broadly similar standard, both wearing metal helmets and carrying swords, the fundamental difference being that the former were unlikely to wear armour in the form of the back and breast. By the 1630s, the shot were diverging in an ever more substantive manner from the pike as reflected in the 1638 *Directions for Musters* which specified that: 'The Pikeman must be armed with a Pike seventeen foot long, head and all; (the diameter of the staff to be one inch, the head to be well steeled, 8 inches long, broad, strong, and sword-pointed; the cheeks 2 foot long, well riveted; the butt-end bound with a ring of iron) a Gorget, Back, Breast, Tassets and Head-Piece, a good Sword of 3 foot long, cutting and stiff-pointed, with Girdle and Hangers. The Musketier must be armed with a good Musket, (the Barrel of 4 foot long, the Bore of 12 bullets in the pound rowling in) a Rest, Bandelier, Head-piece, a good Sword, Girdle and Hangers'.

The Firelocks

Just beginning to come into greater use at the commencement of the period were soldiers armed with the newest type of musket, generically termed 'firelocks'. The contemporary term firelock referred to a musket whose method of ignition was by a flint held in the jaws of a 'cock' striking a 'steel' plate and thus igniting the powder in a pan, which in-turn ignited the main charge in the breech. This form of ignition appears to have been first developed in Holland (although it may also have originated in either Sweden or Germany) in the mid-sixteenth century where the first version was termed by the Dutch a 'Snaphaan' or 'snapping hen' mechanism, which the cock resembled. The snaphance had developed from the wheelock and had a marked similarity in its complex design and ease of damage. There are references to the English forces in Ireland in 1580 being armed with snaphance muskets and warfare in Ireland was particularly suited to the introduction of the firelock in general. By the 1630s the snaphance mechanism had become obsolete, although some were unquestionably still used in the English Civil War, and it had been superseded by three other types of mechanism which were recognisable 'flintlocks', that is, the 'English Lock', the 'Dog Lock', and the 'French Lock'. All three types of mechanism had an 'L' shaped steel or hammer which sat on-top of a frizzen or flash pan, the powder in this being ignited by the flint, held in the jaws of the cock, striking the steel. The three types of lock varied in the detail of the internal mechanism, the English and Dog locks both having external safety catches for the cock, while the French lock had an internal tumbler with two notches in it instead, the first being the 'half-cock' or safety position. While the English Lock was so called because of its popularity in England, it was the French lock mechanism with its

internal safety 'half-cock' which was later in the century to be all but universally adopted as the standard flintlock design in Europe.

During the Civil War, although few of the old snaphances were still in use, the term 'Snaphance' was commonly applied by most contemporaries to all types of flintlock ignited mechanisms. The term firelock was first used to describe the specific military units which would usually be described as being armed with 'Snaphances'.

The reasons for the development of this alternative to the matchlock mechanism were not as obvious as some historians suggest. The standard logic put forward was that the firelock mechanism was more resistant to damp weather and therefore more reliable. While this was to an extent true, the additional expense of the more complex lock and inevitable ease with which it could be damaged off-set this. It must be borne in mind that the matchlock's advantage over a firelock was its very simplicity of ignition, even if the matchlock mechanism was broken, provided the barrel was sound and the match burning, it could still be fired by simply applying the match by hand. The fact that it remained the standard military musket until almost the end of the seventeenth century demonstrates it was not without its inherent strengths. The more compelling logic of the firelock's advantages was in the area of safety, the expense of match-cord and their operational uses. Throughout the history of the matchlock the incidents of musketeers either blowing themselves up by igniting their charges with the match or a more impressive explosion with powder barrels were legion. In addition, a matchlock needed match-cord in considerable quantities and this was

Opposite.

Top left.

An English back-edged rapier made for military use c. 1630. David Edge, Histrionix Living History Group.

Top right.

 A Walloon cavalry trooper's sword c. 1650 as commonly carried by harquebusier. David Edge, Histrionix Living History Group.

Bottom left.

An English 'mortuary-hilt' c. 1640. The grip has lost its original wire covering. David Edge, Histrionix Living History Group.

Bottom right.

A 'Protestant' German straight-bladed infantry hanger c. 1600 with '1414' engraved on blade. 1414 was the talismanic date of the death of the Protestant martyr Huss. David Edge, Histrionix

Top left and right.
Cruso illustrates here a rather unlikely tactic in attempting to adapt the classic 'Reiters' assault of the cuirassiers discharging their pistols before charging to contact. Manoeuvring troops of cuirassier in this manner would have required great training and a lot of luck. The trumpeters of each troop can be clearly seen outside of the attacking bodies. PEW.

expensive, for example, the 1,500 strong Lyme garrison used five hundred-weight of match every twenty-four hours. The firelock, by the very nature of its mechanism, avoided these two factors which were intrinsic to the matchlock. The second factor, the cost of match-cord, meant that the more costly firelock mechanism soon paid for itself in the savings on the cost of match. Finally, the firelock was always ready for immediate action whilst a matchlock needed to be lit, a not inconsiderable process in an ere before the cigarette lighter.

The various advantages of the firelock were concisely set out by Roger Boyle, The Earl of Orrery, in his work *A Treatise of the Art of War* (1677). Orrery not only pointed to the advantages of the mechanism but also indicated the operational role troops armed with such weapons performed: 'I would recommend

the Fire-lock Musket above the Match-lock Musket, for several Reasons; some of which I shall mention. First, It is exceedingly more ready; for with the Fire-lock you have only to Cock, and you are prepared to Shoot; but with your Match-lock; you have several motions, the least of which is as long a performing, as but that one of the other, and oftentimes much more hazardous; besides, if you Fire not the Match-lock Musket as soon as you have blown your Mtach, (which often, especially in Hedge-Fights and in Sieges, you cannot do) you must a second time blow your Match, or the Shes it gathers hinder it from Firing.

'Secondly, The Match is very dangerous, either where Bandeleers are used, or where Soldiers run hastily in Fight to the Budge-barrel, to refill their Bandeleers; I have often seen sad instances thereof.

'Thirdly, Marching in the Nights, to avoid an Enemy, or to surprize one, or to assault a Fortress, the Matches often discover you, and informs the Enemy where you are; whereby you suffer much, and he obtains much.

'Fourthly, In wet weather, the Pan of the Musket being made wide open for awhile, the Rain often deads the Powder, and the Match too; and in windy weather, blows away the Powder, ere the Match can touch the Pan: nay, often in very high Winds, I have seen the

Side view of an Italian cuirassier helmet c.1630. The Trustees of the Wallace Collection, A67.

Sparks blown from the Match, Fire the Musket ere the Soldier meant it; and either thereby lose his Shot, or wound or kill some one before him. Whereas in the Fire-lock the motion is so sudden, that what makes the Cock fall on the Hammer, strikes the Fire, and opens the Pan at once.

'Lastly, To omit many other Reasons, the quantity of Match used in an Army, does much add to the Baggage...'.

The role most often quoted for the first companies of firelocks was as the guard to the artillery train. The military writer Richard Elton reflects this in his comment about the artillery: 'Those which are ordained for their guard to be firelocks or to have snaphances for the avoiding of the danger that might happen by the coal of the match'.

Yet this was far from their only operational use in the mid-seventeenth century and far more companies of firelocks existed than would have been simply required for guarding the various armies artillery trains. Firelocks soon demonstrated various operational advantages over the matchlock, allowing musketeers to approach an enemy unseen, saving vast

quantities of match when on sentry duty and always being ready for instant action. Certainly they were favoured in Ireland even before the outbreak of the English Civil War. A number of officers who had served there stressed the firelock's value over the matchlock. Essentially, the nature of warfare in Ireland, with its many ambushes, sieges, garrisons and other small actions all favoured their increasing deployment. The recognition of the usefulness of the firelock in Ireland can be judged by the planned organisation of the regiments due to be sent to Ireland in early 1642 where every fifth company of foot was to be armed with them. The senior English regiment in Ireland, the Lord Lieutenant's Regiment, had 400 hundred firelocks on its strength alongside its normal 1500 men armed with matchlock and pike. These firelocks had certainly arrived by late March 1642 and may have been in addition to the two independent companies under Captains Thomas Sandford and Francis Langley already listed as serving in Ireland.

In England, during the Civil War, some of the companies of firelocks that fought on the Royalist side were drawn from the army in Ireland, such as Sandford's and Langley's. There were, however, earlier companies of firelocks which were specifically raised for the King's and Parliament's armies in England. For

the King there was William Legge's Firelocks who do appear to have been originally raised for the traditional role of guarding the artillery train and were then attached to the King's Lifeguard of Foot. On Parliament's side Essex had 100 firelocks under Lieutenant-General de Boyes to guard the train in October 1642, while General James Wemyss (a former Master Gunner of England) raised two companies of blue-coated firelocks to guard Waller's artillery train in October 1643. Prince Rupert, from late 1643, had his own red-coated Lifeguard armed with Firelocks as did his brother, Prince Maurice. Later in the war, a number of other firelock units were operating in the Welsh marches and Severn Valley, Chirke's Firelocks, also known as Sir John Watt's Foot, being an example. It also appears that a number of standard Royalist infantry regiments were issued with a proportion of firelocks, Colonel James Proger's Foot had some in September 1644 at an action at Monmouth and the

Royalist Ordnance Papers record that on 13th February 1645 there were issued, 'Three score Snaphance unto Sir Henry Bard..'.

The use of firelocks in England does not appear to have been markedly different from that in Ireland. A writer with far greater experience than Orrery, Sir James Turner, who had served on the Continent, in Ireland, Scotland and England, wrote in *Pallas Armata* about the advantages for firelocks in particular circumstances and appears to reflect the contemporary opinion that firelocks were valuable for special service beyond just guarding the artillery train,

'It is impossible to hide burning Matches so well in the night-time especially if there be any wind, (though there be covers made of white Iron, like extinguishers* purposely for that end) but that some will be seen by a vigilant enemy, and thereby many secret enterprises are lost......the sight whereof hath ruin'd many good designs'.

(*Extinguishers. On many occasions the lighted match of matchlock muskets had given warning of surprise attack to garrisons and the like. In an attempt to solve this inherent problem with match, the Prince of Orange had invented a tin pipe about a foot long to

Detached cuirassier breastplate only, showing musket proof, arsenal number and fixings for long tassets. The Trustees of the Wallace Collection, A65.

Detached cuirassier backplate and culet disassembled. The Trustees of the Wallace Collection, A65.

contain the match and hide its light: it had holes in the side like a flute to let in the air and prevent the match from being extinguished. While this worked, it was cumbersome to say the least).

The 'secret enterprises' in England usually involved assaults on fortifications. For example, on 13th December 1643, Captain Thomas Sandford led 8 of his firelocks in scaling the steep rocks which fell precipitously away from one side of Beeston Castle and were believed to have been impregnable. Another Royalist unit of firelocks which led a number of assaults on fortifications were Prince Rupert's Lifeguard of Firelocks. In January 1645 they led an abortive assault on the defences of Abingdon while on 30th May 1645 they led the successful assault on the walls of Leicester. Their firelocks also made them ideal as garrison troops which was demonstrated when they were recorded as being with Rupert when he marched out after surrendering Bristol on 11th September 1645, '...his Life Guard of fire-locks came forth, all in red coats before him...'.

As with the Royalist army, Parliament's companies

Bottom left and right.
Detached cuirassier breastplate only, showing musket proof, arsenal number and fixings for long tassets. The Trustees of the Wallace Collection, A65.

of firelocks were found both guarding the artillery train as part of the Ordnance and as specialist companies in otherwise standard infantry regiments. The latter were found in commanding officers' regiments, for example the Lord Generall's and the Lieutenant-General of the Ordnance's regiments were viewed, as were Prince Rupert's and Maurice's Lifeguard's of Firelock's, as elite bodies. Their specific function was to provide a guard for the personage of

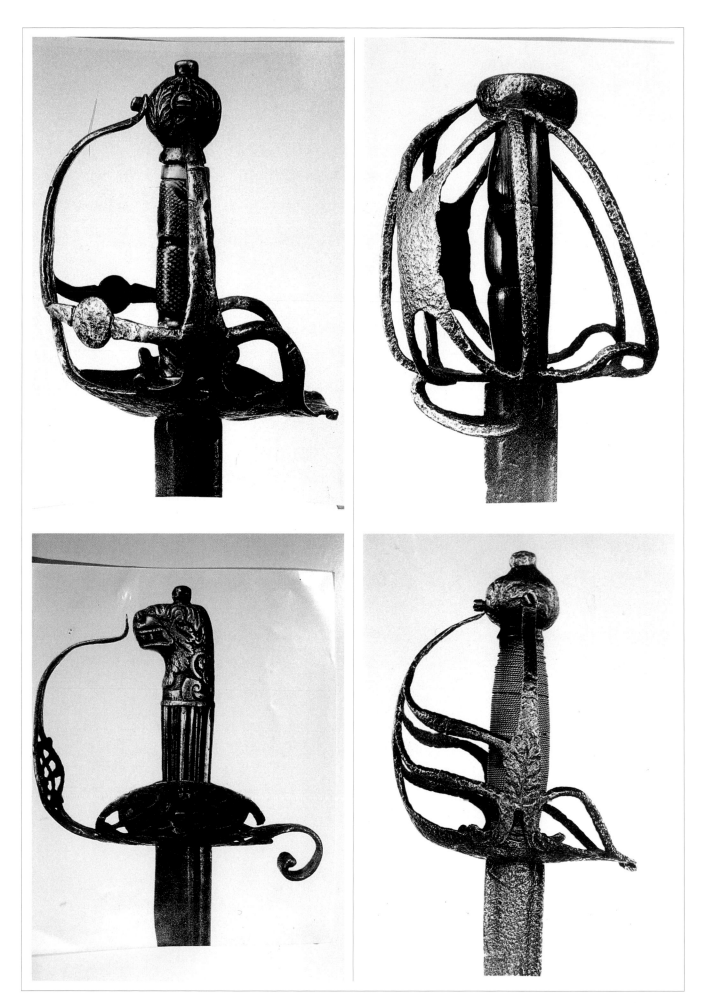

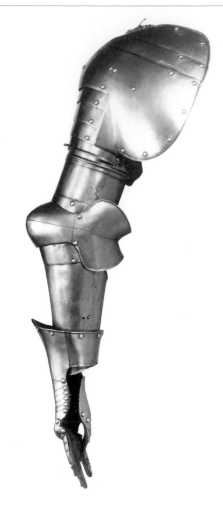

Top left and right; Opposite left.

Detached cuirassier arm harness, side plus both back and front. The Trustees of the Wallace Collection, A65.

the commander where their firelocks would ensure instant reaction to any threat whilst also being available for storming fortifications, general out-post work and even ambushes.

While there are no surviving details on the specific organisation and equipment for Royalist companies of firelocks, there are for Parliament's forces that were assigned to guard the Artillery Train. Firstly, there was the company of firelocks under de Boyes under the command of the companies senior Lieutenant, Richard Price. The rest of the company consisted of an ensign, 2 sergeants, 3 corporals, 2 drummers and 66 men, the company being short of its regulation strength of 100 men. On the 10th of October 1642, they were issued standard uniform coats and were otherwise equipped as a normal company of foot with an ensign, halberts, 2 drums, 100 firelocks and 100 swords. Secondly, when the New Model Army was raised in early 1645 it included two companies of firelocks under the command of Major John Desborough attached as guards to the Artillery Train. Composed from the companies in Essex's, Waller's and

Manchester's armies, those of the former were still wearing their tawny coats when they fought at Naseby. These firelocks proved to be a valuable asset there where they famously held off Prince Rupert's horse from looting the baggage train drawn up in the rear of the army, and they are clearly represented in the famous drawing of Naseby in Joshua Sprigge's 'Anglia Redivia' in the bottom left hand corner. Their organisation and equipment was almost identical to that of de Boyes' earlier company. Each of the two companies consisted of 1 captain, 1 lieutenant, 1 ensign, 2 sergeants, 3 corporals and 100 firelocks (there was no mention of drummers). As with the rest of the New Model foot, they were ultimately issued red coats.

The Horse

The establishment for a regiment of horse could vary significantly as no specific directions were laid down as to regulation strengths. Most military manuals were prefaced on a theoretical standard of between 400 to 500 troopers plus officers, divided into six troops for administrative purposes. The manuals had troops ranging in strength between 80 for fully armoured cuirassiers to 60 men for the lighter harquebusiers. In practice regiments could be both much larger and

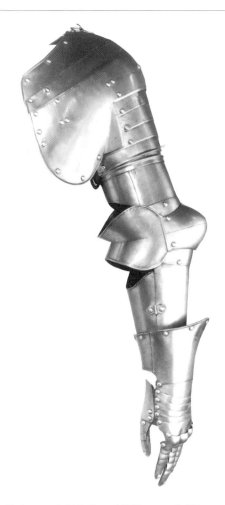

smaller. Prior to 1642, Lord Wharton's Horse, raised as harquebusiers for service in Ireland in late 1641, fielded 80 men in Wharton's own troop, with each of his captain's at 70 strong. At the commencement of the civil war the only specification for Parliament's army was that each troop, which were raised separately rather than as regiments, had to muster a minimum of 40 men. Having said this, Essex's Lifeguard recorded 100 men per troop. Later in the war, in the Eastern Association, Cromwell commanded fourteen troops in his regiment, the Earl of Manchester's fielded eleven whilst Charles Fleetwood's numbered six and Quartermaster-General Vermuyden's an almost standard five. In addition, by September 1644, the average strength of an Eastern Association troop was 99 men. At least for Essex's army, the establishment of regiments of horse was standardised on paper in March 1644 when an ordinance stipulated that there should be 3,000 men organised into six regiments, each of six troops. The colonel's troop was to be 100 men plus officers, each captain's troop to be 80 men plus officers. In practice, variations in troop strength continued until Essex's army was absorbed by the New Model in early 1645. On the Royalist side, Prince Rupert's regiment regularly fielded ten troops, although each only averaged some 50 troopers.

Having said this, his personal Lifeguard averaged 150 men divided into two troops.

At the other end of the spectrum, many regiments had understrength troops and fielded well below the standard six troops. Amongst the generally stronger Eastern Association regiments, Sir John Norwich's regiment fielded just three troops whilst on the Marston Moor campaign Fairfax's troops averaged just 25 men apiece. Amongst the Royalists, Major Legge's troop at Edgehill mustered only 15 troopers and at the Aldbourne Chase muster on 10th April 1644 the average troop strength was only 44. Generally, Royalist regiments were weaker than comparable Parliamentary formations.

As for commissioned officers, the staff of an average regiment included the colonel, a lieutenant-colonel, (although in Parliamentarian regiments only the stronger regiments and those of a general officer such as that of the Earl of Essex included a lieutenant-colonel), and a major. As with the staff of an infantry regiment, there was an additional number of specialists, including a clerk, a Chirurgeon (surgeon) and for some Parliamentary regiments, a preacher.

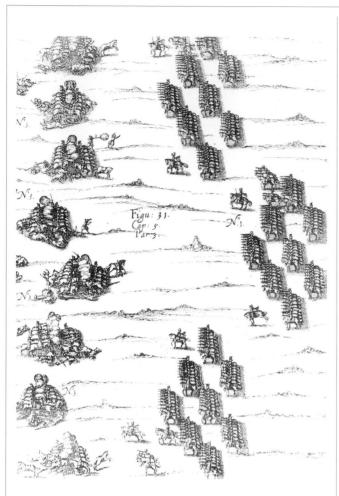

Top left and right.

Wallhausen's illustrations of charging cavalry more accurately reflects the tactical formations employed by Civil War harquebusiers. PEW.

The commissioned officers of each troop consisted of a captain (a captain-lieutenant for the colonel's troop), lieutenant, cornet and a quartermaster (only the quartermasters of cavalry regiments were commissioned), the non-commissioned officers being 3 corporals and 2 trumpeters (ranked as corporals), with the specialists including a clerk, a saddler and a farrier.

On the battlefield, the troops were organised into squadrons or 'divisions'. If up to strength, two troops would constitute a squadron, although this could increase in direct proportion to the paucity of numbers fielded by each troop. If following contemporary Swedish practice, the squadrons would be drawn up three ranks deep, if retaining the more antiquated Dutch or 'Reiter' model, six ranks deep. Judging by the initial clashes as Powick Bridge and Edgehill, Parliament began the war following the latter practice of advancing at the trot, with each rank successively halting to give fire with their pistols or carbines before filing away to the rear to reload whilst the next rank gave fire. This tactic assumed the opponent would equally halt to deliver fire and the charge was reserved for when firepower had effectively broken the opposition. Thanks to Rupert, the Royalist horse adopted the Swedish practice whereby his troopers charged home, reserving their fire for the melee and pursuit. As it had for the previous decade or more on the Continent, this immediately demonstrated its decisiveness by literally sweeping Parliament's stationary troops away. As often in war, the losers were fast learners and the opening clashes of 1643 witnessed Cromwell, Fairfax and many other Parliamentarians demonstrating that they had learned the painful lesson. Ultimately, these officers outmatched Rupert with the addition of discipline and control to this tactic, as so decisively demonstrated at Marston Moor and Naseby.

Still very much the social superiors of the infantry, the horse fell into two categories, cuirassier and harquebusier. The cuirassier was viewed as the superior of the two, regiments of such heavily armoured horse being common in Continental armies. Hexham, writing in *Principles* on the eve of the Civil War, described the ideal of such troops: 'In a cuirassier then is required, that he be a man of an able body, who is mounted upon a strong, and a lustie horse, that he

Wallhausen illustrates a body of dismounted dragoons (one can see their horses at the rear) including both pike and shot. In practice English dragoons were all musketeers. As can be seen, the dragoons were equipped as standard infantry, including full size colours. PEW.

Also from Wallhausen, this dragoon is equipped as a standard musketeer of 1616, with bandoleer, sword and helmet. Having said this, his specialist role as a dragoon is reflected in the fact that his short barrelled matchlock musket is slung over his shoulder on a belt attached to either end and he wears buttoned gaiters on his lower legs. PEW.

hath on a good buff-gerkin, a short sword, or Coutlase by his side, a skarff about his armes, and bodie of his princes coullour, to distinguish him from his Ennemie coullour upon any service, or in the daie of battel.

'He ought to be mounted upon a strong, and a lustie horse, or Gelding, which is fiveteene palmes high...and likewise to be provided with a good Sadle, and Bridle, with two good pistolls hanging at his sadle bowe, in two strong pistoll Cases, the length of the pistoll barrils, being at the least foure and twenty ynches long, carrying a bullet of twentie in the pound, and of 24 which will roule in to his pistoll.

'For his Armes about his bodie, he is first armed with a close helmet or a Cask pistoll proofe upon his head, 2. with a Gorget about his neck, 3. His brest and back peeces, which ought to be pistoll proofe, 4. His Pauldrons and vambraces his Guard de reines, 5. His gauntles, 6. his tassets or thigh peeces reaching from his girdle beneath his knees, and (as is said) two pistols hanging at his saddle, and thus a Curassier is armed de

cap en pied at all points even from the head to the foote.'

In fact, although some in England aspired to such troopers, the expense of providing the armour and equipment meant that in practice only a handful of such formations were raised, mostly at the commencement of the conflict by Parliament. This possibly reflected Parliament's greater resources as such troops required large horses to carry the weight and as Monck wrote in 1644, 'there are not many Countries that do afford Horses fit for the Service of Cuirassiers', an observation easily transferable to the King's straightened circumstances. There were just three such troops in Essex's army in 1642 serving as his Lifeguard whilst Waller's army fielded the more famous 'lobsters' of Sir Arthur Haselrigg. There might have been at least one such formation in the King's army a little later in the war as the Royalist Ordinance papers record for 2nd May 1644 the issue

A Mid-War Musketeer, 1643-44.

This musketeer reflects the general appearance of both the King's and Parliament's men once their respective war efforts had entered into their stride. Most soldiers by mid-1643 were receiving suits of clothes, those for the Royalists issued in July 1643, supplied by Thomas Bushell, being described by Anthony Wood as '...all the common soldiers then at Oxford were newe apparrelled, some all in red, coates, breeches, & mounteers; & some all in blewe'. The coat and breeches would have been made from pre-shrunk wool broadcloth or kersey which was also used to cover the thirty or so buttons of the coat and six of the breeches. The lining was of a lighter wool, revealed by the rolled back cuff. Although illustrated here wearing a black felt broad brimmed hat, a version of the more common Montero manufactured in blue wool broadcloth appears at the top of the picture. The formal issue of clothes would often include shirts of lockram or Osnaburg linen and cotton or woollen grey knitted stockings, a pair of leather shoes completing the ensemble. In terms of equipment this musketeer is well provided for with a collar of bandoliers with some twelve charges of either wood or tin plate, a pattern sword and a snapsack for personal items, food and extra stockings and shirts.

The two primary types of musket, the matchlock and firelock, appear to the soldier's right, including tools for cleaning and maintenance. Although the standard barrel length was four feet, shorter and lighter 'bastard' muskets with barrels of around three foot six inches became common as the war progressed. Below is a collar of bandoliers with a leather flap to prevent rain penetration. To the soldier's left are examples of three types of pattern sword along with both waist and shoulder belts. Finally, above the soldiers' right shoulder is a snapsack, commonly made from leather or cotton canvas. For the common soldier, all metal fittings were normally of iron. *Painting by Christa Hook.*

of, '60 Case of Pistolls with Holsters, and 40 Carabines ...., and the same proportion of Sadles and Bits...for the Arming of a Troope of One Hundred Curasiers to be r[aised] for Colonell Blagge..'. Whether this troop was ultimately raised and was indeed fully armoured cuirassiers or simply a mis-termed troop of harquebusier was not recorded.

As it was, the actual battlefield experiences of Parliament's cuirassier formations soon revealed the disadvantages of such latter day armoured knights, both on the individual level and as coherent battlefield units. Having served as a cuirassier in Essex's Lifeguard at Edgehill, Edmund Ludlow recorded in his memoirs that, 'Being dismounted I could not without difficulty recover on horseback being loaded with cuirassiers arms, as the rest of the guard also were'. For the Royalists, Sir Edmund Verney bluntly commented just prior to his death at Edgehill, '...it will kill a man to serve in a whole cuirass. I am resolved to use nothing but back breast and gauntlet. If I had a pott for the head that were pistol proof it may be that I would use it, if it were light, but my whole helmet will be of no use to me at all'. Verney was as good as his word as he was killed at Edgehill wearing neither armour or a buff-coat.

Any expectation that their armour would allow them to retain the traditional Reiter tactic of the deeper six rank formation and relying on firepower to defeat an opponent was conclusively proved to be fatuous at Roundway Down in 1643. Haselrigg's lobsters were ridden down by the lightly armoured Royalist horse and dramatically driven over a cliff. Richard Atkyns recorded that: 'We lost no time, but marched towards the enemy, who stood towards the top of the hill;....then forlorn-hopes out of each army were drawn out, and the Lord Wilmott's Major, Paul Smith commanded ours, who did it with that gallantry, that he beat them into the very body of their left wing, and put them out of order; which we took advantage of, and immediately charged the whole body; the charge was so sudden that I had hardly time to put on my arms, we advanced a full trot 3 deep, and kept in order; the enemy kept their station, and their right wing of horse being cuirassiers, were I'm sure five, if not six deep, in so close order, that Punchinello himself had been there, could not have gotten in to them.

'All the horse on the left hand of Prince Maurice his regiment, had none to charge; we charging the very utmost man of their right wing...for though they were above twice our numbers; they being six deep, in close order and we but three deep, and open (by reason of our sudden charge) we were without them at both ends....No man ever charged better than ours did that day'.

Having said this, Atkyns, in relating another troopers story of how he had captured Haselrigg, demonstrated that, at least for the commander of the lobsters, his armour was both sword and pistol proof and that the only way to bring such a cuirassier down was to kill his horse: 'When he wheeled off, I pursued him,...and in six score yards I came up to him, and discharged the other pistol at him, and I'm sure I hit his head, for I touched it before I gave fire, and it amazed him at that present, but he was too well armed all over for a pistol bullet to do him any hurt, having...a headpiece (I am confident) musket proof, his sword had two edges and a ridge in the middle, and

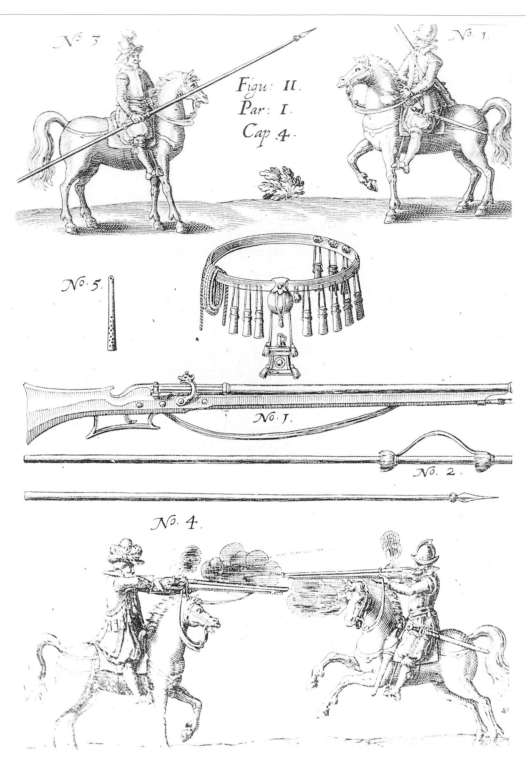

Wallhausen illustrated the equipment of dragoons, including the leather strap on the musket. All the dragoons are clothed as standard infantry, without even riding boots. Note that the figure at the bottom right hand is a harquebusier. PEW.

mine [was] a strong tuck;...I came up to him again...and struck by him a god while, and tried him from head to the saddle, and could not penetrate him, nor do him any hurt...resolved to attempt nothing further than to kill his horse; all this time we were together hand to fist. In this nick of time came up Mr Holmes to my assistance...and went up to him with great resolution, and felt him before he discharged his pistol, and though I saw him hit him, 'twas but a flea-biting to him; whilst he charged him, I employed myself in killing his horse, and ran him into several places, and upon the faltering of his horse his headpiece opened behind, and I gave him a prick in the neck...then came in Captain Buck a gentleman of my troop, and discharged his pistol upon him also, but with the same success as before...by this time his horse began to be faint with bleeding, and fell off from his rate'.

In the event, Haselrigg was rescued before being

This dragoon is taken from the frontispiece of Cruso's work and bears an uncanny resemblance, albeit from a different angle, to Wallhausen's dragoon, including the musket slung over the shoulder. PEW.

On the left hand side of Sprigg's famous map of Naseby in *Anglia Redivia* Okey's Regiment of Dragoons can just be made out firing from behind the hedge on Rupert's right wing. PEW.

carted off as a prisoner, although this episode did give rise to one of the very few examples of humour by the King for:

'This story being related to the late King [Charles I]...his answer was "Had he been victualled as well as fortified, he might have endured a siege of seven years, &c." '

Subsequently, cuirassier formations vanished from the English battlefield, although individual officers continued to wear the better quality suits.

Wilmott's troopers, including Atkyns, who so brutally demonstrated the pointlessness of cuirassier armour, were equipped, as were the vast majority of horse in the Civil War, as harquebusiers, effectively categorised as light horse. Vernon, in *The Young Horseman*, detailed their equipment as: 'The Harquebus and Carbines arming is chiefly offensive, his defensive arms as only an open Caske or Headpiece, a back and breast with a buff-coat under his arms. His offensive arms are a good harquebus, [or] a carbine hanging on his right side in a belt by a swivel, a flask and cartridge case, and spanners and good firelock pistols in holsters. At his saddle a good stiffe sword sharp pointed and a good poll axe in his hand'.

Their advantage over the cuirassiers was identified after the war by a writer known only as 'JB' who added to William Barriffe's manual, *Military Discipline*, for its 1661 edition a section on horse, writing: 'But our late English wars neglected....cuirassiers and lancers making use of Harquebusiers. Armed only with a breast back and casque or pott for defence, a case of pistols short, and a carbine, hanging by a belt and swivel on his right side, of 2 or 2 1/2 foot the length of the barrel and a good sword. Many troops and regiments only with sword and Pistol armed, their encounterings being not after the ancient manner of firing at a distance and wheeling off, which hath been found to be of dangerous consequence, but to fire at near distance their swords hanging at their wrists by a string, and with their sword points charging through the adverse troops'.

Before leaving the topic of infantry and cavalry

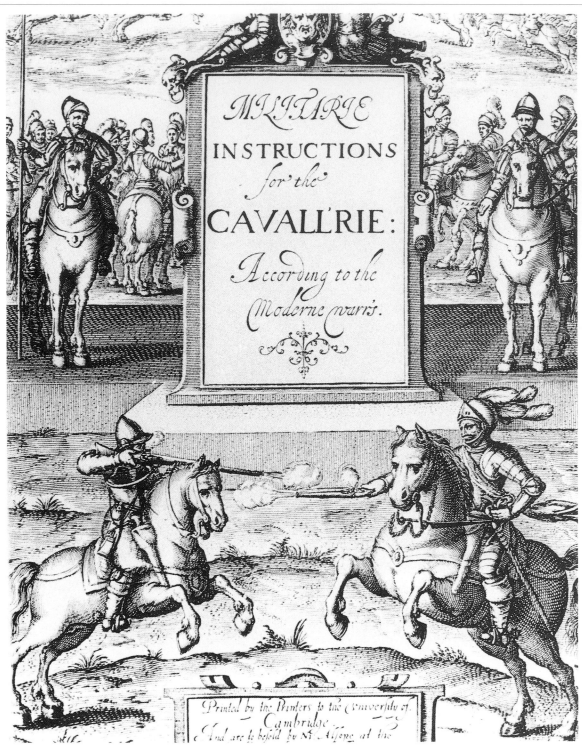

This title piece from Cruso illustrated dragoons either side of the wording at the top with a harquebusier and cuirassier respectively at the foot. PEW.

equipment, probably one of the greatest changes which was to occur during the conflicts of the 1640s as a result of empirical experience on the battlefield was the sharp decline in the general use of armour. As previously related, the once respected cuirassiers soon vanished forever from the rolls of any English army. The armour worn by the harquebusier and humble pikeman, although continued for longer, equally came to be seen as less important. Even before the war, Cruso had commented on a growing reluctance amongst soldiers to wear armour due to its weight and a belief it was a sign of cowardice. Although Cruso urged the retention of armour, the experience of war soon proved right the ordinary soldier's intuition towards armour. The reason for this was simple, the musket. It had been true that some of the high quality steel armours of the previous century, particularly those from Italy, had been capable of either stopping or sufficiently slowing the musket ball of that era, propelled as they were by poorly mixed powders. Two fundamental factors though had changed by the mid seventeenth century. Firstly, the need to equip larger armies for longer meant that state treasuries could no longer afford to equip their troops in steel armour. The vast majority of back and breasts, both for horse and pike, were thus cheaply manufactured in iron. This consequently imposed a restriction on the thickness of that armour given the greater weight ratio of iron to steel for the same degree of protection. Particularly for a pikeman, who lacked a horse to help bear the burden, if he was not to sink under the sheer weight of his iron armour there was a limit to a thickness of a few millimetres. Secondly, the mixing and quality of powder had dramatically improved during the sixteenth century. New manufacturing technologies, particularly the corning of powder, dramatically increased its power and hence the velocity of the musket ball it propelled.

Modern tests carried out at the Landeszeughaus at Graz in Austria and at the Tower Armouries in England using original weapons and armour have conclusively demonstrated what many contemporaries knew. Essentially, whilst protection against sword and

Although their impact on the battlefield was normally marginal, no self-respecting army would have been without field guns. In the foreground is the powder chest. English Heritage.

pike, the vast majority of the ordinary soldiers' iron armour was incapable of stopping a musket ball from within 100 to 150 yards. Higher quality officers' armour, for example that worn by Haselrigg, was certainly proof against a small calibre pistol ball, even at point blank range. At Graz and the Tower, however, test firing seventeenth century muskets and carbines revealed a lead ball at 40 yards had an energy value at impact of around 2,800 joules, dropping to around 1,500 joules at 100 yards. The contemporary iron breastplates could easily be penetrated at between 400 and 600 joules, whilst a steel one at around 1000. Essentially a musket ball could punch through the former like butter. Once foot soldiers realised iron armour could not stop a musket ball, it simply became a heavy encumbrance, hampering mobility in combat. For the horse, a good buff coat could as effectively turn a sword as well as any iron back and breast. Even officers in possession of better quality armour found it an encumbrance: for the assault on Shelford House in 1645, 'Colonel Hutchinson put off a very good suit of armour which he had, which being musket proof was so heavy that it heated him, and so would not be persuaded by his friends to wear anything but his buff-coat'.

Having said this, whilst lighter, high quality buff-coats were certainly not a cheaper option. A good

quality set of harquebusiers armour consisting of back, breast, pot and gauntlet could be had in 1642 for as little as £2, whilst in 1640, John Tubervill wrote to his father-in-law John Willoughby, 'For your buff-coat I have looked after, and the price: they are exceedingly dear, not a good one to be gotten under £10, a very poor one for five or six pounds'. This ensured they were the prerogative of officers and the better equipped horse. Basically, as the war dragged on, fewer and fewer pikemen wore armour and not being able to afford buff-coats simply dressed in clothes identical to that of the musketeers. While harquebusiers continued to wear armour, this was because it was the cheaper option to protect against sword and pike cuts and their mounts helped offset the additional weight. Underneath they wore cheap, thin leather coats, essentially to prevent the armour chaffing rather than for protection from an enemy's sword.

The Dragoons

Crossing the boundary between the horse and foot were a relatively new category of soldier, the dragoon. There is no clear agreement on when the concept of a mounted musketeer had evolved although it was undoubtedly towards the end of the sixteenth century in France. Certainly the French army fighting in Piedmont between 1552 and 1559 under Marshal de Brissac had utilised mounted harquebusiers whilst during the late sixteenth century French wars of religion the Huguenot forces made extensive use of mounted musketeers. By the time Wallhausen wrote his *Manuale Militare* in 1616 they were becoming a recognised element of a modern European army, the Dutch having had dragoons proper in 1606 and the Swedes in 1611. Although some contemporary writers tended to suggest equipment more in keeping with the horse, in fact they were firmly part of the infantry, being clothed and equipped solely for that role. They were not expected to fight from horseback, rather their small and cheap mounts, fitted with cheap saddles, were solely for mobility to enable them to keep up with the regiments of horse on the march, dismounting to provide firepower for them in action. They were equally used in the vanguard as pathfinders, clearing roads, securing bridges, essentially as maids of all work. Taking his lead from Wallhausen, Robert Ward wrote in *Animadversions* in 1639: 'The Dragoones are no lese than a foote company, consisting of Pikes and Muskets, only for their quicker expedition they are mounted upon horses. They are of greate use for the guarding of passages and fordes, in regard of their swiftnesses they

may prevent the enemies foote, and gaine places of advantage to hinder their passage.

'Their Pikes are to have thongs of leather about the middle of them, for the easier carriage of them.

'The Muskets are to have a broad strong belt fastened to the stocke of them, well neere from one end to the other, whereby he hangs it upon his backe when he rideth, holding his match and bridle in his left hand: any horse if he be swifte will performe this service, in regard they alight and doe their service a foote; so that when tenne men alight, the eleventh holdeth their horses, so that to every troope of 120 there is 132 men allowed'.

In practice there was little evidence to suggest any English dragoons were issued pikes. Rather they were purely mounted shot. Whilst originally armed with matchlocks, as Monck wrote in 1644, they were ideally armed with the newer firelocks:

'A musquet, or a good Snapance to a Musquet Barrel; the which I hold much better for Dragoon-Service, being upon occasion they may be able to make use of their Snapances on Horse-back, and upon any Service in night they may go undiscovered. He must have also a belt to hang his Musquet in, with a pair of Bandaliers and a good long Tuck, with a Belt'.

In fact, their muskets were specifically termed 'dragoons', almost certainly referring to their shorter length for ease of carriage when mounted. Whilst the standard length of an infantry musket barrel, be it a matchlock or firelock, remained four feet (although shorter 'bastard' muskets were becoming common), dragoon firelocks had just three foot barrels. Finally, driving home as it were that dragoons primarily fought on foot, Monck added to their list of equipment 'Swine-feathers' (also known as 'Swedish feathers'). These were wooden poles fitted with pike heads at both ends enabling one end to be driven into the ground so that the protruding end would fend off enemy cavalry.

The Artillery

The final military arm was the artillery. The professional gunner and his guns were a recognised part of any self-respecting army of the day. Although cannon in the first half of the seventeenth century were clumsy, difficult to move and of limited effect, (except in sieges), an artillery train was considered a vital part of the army. This was despite its great cost, for as Clarendon bemoaned of the King's far from adequate train prior to Edgehill, it '...is a spunge that can never be filled or satisfied'. The guns of the train though were largely designated for siege operations, field artillery still being very much in its infancy although both siege and field artillery were to be found in any substantial train. The guns were categorised by the weight of their shot, although strictly speaking there was no definitively recognised standardisation.

	Weight of shot	Calibre of barrel	Weight of Gun	Crew	Horse team
Cannon Royal	63lb.	8in.	8000lb.	16	90
Whole Cannon	47lb.	7in.	7000lb.	12	70
Demi-Cannon	27lb.	6in.	6000lb.	10	60
Culverin	15lb.	5in.	4000lb.	8	50
Demi-Culverin	9lb.	4½in.	3600lb.	7	36
Saker	5½lb.	3½in.	2500lb.	6	24
Minion	4lb.	3in.	1500lb.	4	20
Falcon	2¼lb.	2¾in.	700lb.	2	16
Falconet	1¼lb.	2in.	210lb.	"	10
Robinet	¾lb.	1¼in.	120lb	"	8
Base	1/2lb.	1in.	90lb.	"	6

It should be noted that the number of horses listed above required by each gun included both those needed to pull the gun and those pulling wagons carrying powder, shot and equipment. Equally, the crew listed for each gun was divided into gunners and matrosses (assistants). Thus for a demi-cannon there were 4 gunners and 6 matrosses, for a demi-culverin 3 gunners and 4 matrosses and for a saker 2 gunners and 4 matrosses. A mortar required 2 gunners, 6 matrosses and 20 horses.

The ranges of the above when firing solid iron shot varied greatly. For the culverin, which was a standard siege gun, it had a maximum reach of some 2,650 yards. The demi-culverin, probably the largest piece found on any battlefield although normally reserved for use in sieges, could reach 2,400 yards. The standard field piece, the saker, had a range of 2,170 yards, whilst the smaller falcon could reach 1,920 yards.

In terms of personal equipment and clothes, both the officers and men of the train of artillery, particularly the civilian carters, essentially remained in their civilian attire or were clothed as the foot. Items of additional equipment were issued. For personal protection, 5 gunners and 12 matrosses of Rupert's train of artillery at Lichfield in March 1643 received long poleaxes whilst 2 wheelwrights were issued swords.

The Civil War and subsequent conflicts were littered with sieges and, provided the appropriate guns

Whilst still in its infancy on the battlefield, artillery played a crucial role in sieges and many learned works dealt in detail with its science. PEW.

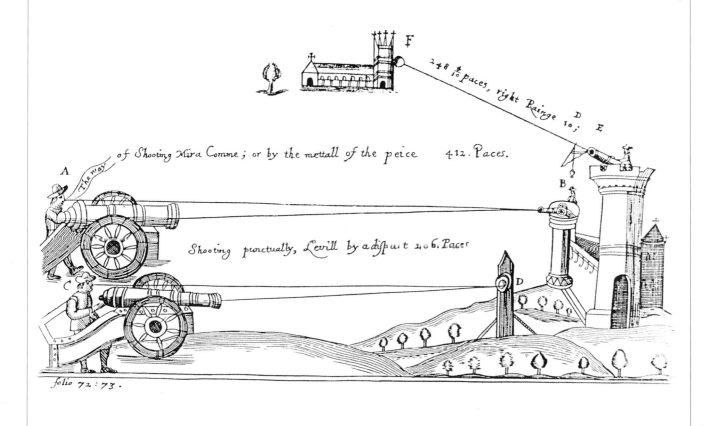

Gunner's linstock, probably Italian c.1600. The Trustees of the Wallace Collection, A1327.

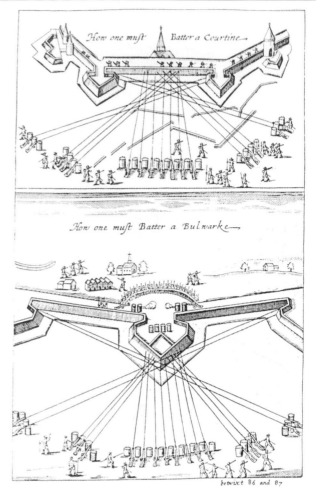

Top right.
The Compleat Gunner illustrates the use of gabions in constructing protected batteries to bombard and breach the standard bastion of the day. PEW.

were available, their use could rapidly reduce the vast majority of existing medieval castle and city walls to rubble. At Sherborne Castle in 1645, 'The great Guns began to play about eleven of the clock, and before six had made a breach in the middle of the wall, that ten men a breast might enter, and had beaten down one of the Towers which much disheartened the enemy'. Fully appreciating the hitting power of such guns, most civil war fortifications were surrounded by earthen ramparts which proved remarkably effective at absorbing shot and usually required either a bloody frontal assault to overcome or a traditional siege to starve the garrison out.

The only alternative was to employ another category of weapon, the mortar. These squat, short barrelled, wide bored weapons were able to use a high trajectory to drop an explosive projectile out of the

Opposite.
Top left.
These colours were captured by the New Model Army at Neseby. Their horizontal stripes are rather old fashioned being a common design prior to the war, particularly amongst the trained bands. Partizan Press.

Top right.
The four senior officers' colours of Sir James Pennyman's Regiment adhered to common practice. The colonel's colour being a simple green field, the lieutenant-colonel with just the St.George's canton, the major with a single red pile wavy and the senior captain two. Each subsequent company added an additional red pile wavy. Partizan Press.

Botttom left.
The colours of Colonel Charles Fairfax's Regiment were blue with white stars. As was very common, the number of stars corresponded to the seniority of the respective company. Partizan Press.

Bottom right.
Less common, but far from unique was the gyronny system, here illustrated by Sir Allan Apsley's colours. The three senior officers' colours were of a standard design, the captain's colours designated by alternating diagonals. Partizan Press.

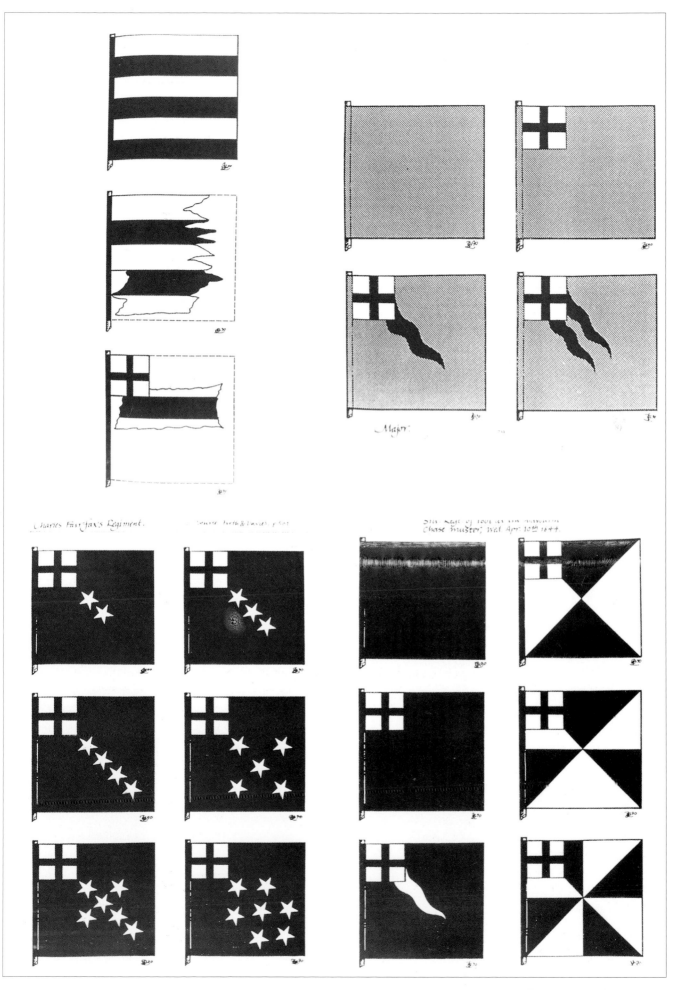

sky. The calibre of mortars varied greatly, although examples survive ranging in size from 15 inches down to 8 inches. Equally distinguishing it from the gun were shells, which rather than being solid, were hollow iron spheres filled with powder with a slow burning fuse to ignite the shell upon landing. This of course relied upon the skill of the gunner to correctly cut the fuse to the required length before lighting it and then dropping it into the barrel before launch. This aspect of its workings ensured there were numerous examples of shells landing whilst their fuses were still fizzing, sometimes allowing brave souls to douse them before exploding. At the siege of Gloucester in 1643 a mortar shell, 'fell into the street near the South gate, but a woman coming by with a payle of water threw the water thereon, and extinguished the phuse [fuse] thereof, so that it did not break'. None the less, if correctly used they could have both a great physical and morale damaging effect. At Lathom House in 1644 they, 'struck most fear with the garrison...The mortar peece was that that troubled us all. The little ladyes had stomack to digest canon, but the stoutest souldiers had noe heart for granadoes. The mortar peece...had frightened 'em from meat and sleepe'.

Despite this, many crumbling stone walls were saved by the simple lack of adequate roads. The many muddy tracks which passed for major avenues of transport often meant heavy guns and mortars had to be moved by water. If a garrison was sufficiently inaccessible, even mediocre Norman masonry could keep the enemy at bay.

Due to the weight of the hefty wooden carriages, the battlefield use of guns was restricted. By the early seventeenth century, field guns were an accepted feature on battlefields and despite popular misconceptions, they were capable of substantial and sustained rates of fire. Yet they were limited by the weight of the wooden carriages required to support the thick iron and brass barrels. Once these lumbering pieces were dragged into position they were simply not capable of being moved if the flow of battle left them behind. Apart from opening barrages, it was only occasionally that guns had played a decisive role in events. At most of the major confrontations of the Civil War, including Edgehill, Marston Moor and Naseby, the guns threw a few initial shot before both sides fell on, thus effectively masking their respective artillery for the remainder of the battle. In fact at Naseby, so rapid was the Royalist advance that their guns were not even in position and did not participate other than to fall as booty into Parliament's hands. Yet there were exceptions. At Langport in July 1645

Sprigge described how: '...our Ordnance began to play (a good while before the foot engaged) doing great execution upon the body of the enemies Army, both horse and foot, who stood in good order upon the hill (about musket shot from the passe) and forcing them to draw off their Ordnance, and their horse to remove their ground'.

On the Continent though, particularly under Gustavus, the use of field guns on the battlefield had advanced. Seeking to provide mobile field pieces, in 1627 the Swedes had adopted the invention of a Swiss mathematician, Master Philip Eberhard, the 'leather gun'. While various models existed, they threw a shot ranging from 3lb to 4lb. Generally they were constructed of bronze or brass tubes, about one third of an inch thick at the muzzle, strengthened by white or tinned iron wire wrapped around it. This was then bound with hemp cord an inch and a quarter thick which was treated with plaster of Paris, and the whole covered in shrunken-on leather. A contemporary observer commented that, 'These leather pieces are of very great use, and very easie and light of carriage. One horse may draw a peece, which will carry a bullet of a pound and half weight, and doe execution very

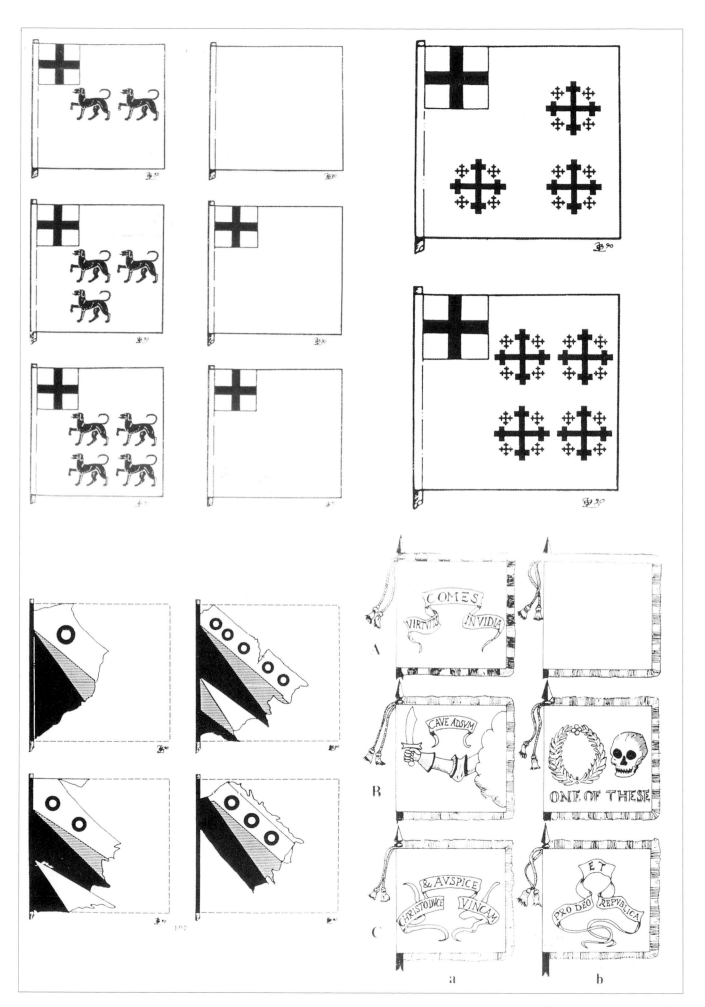

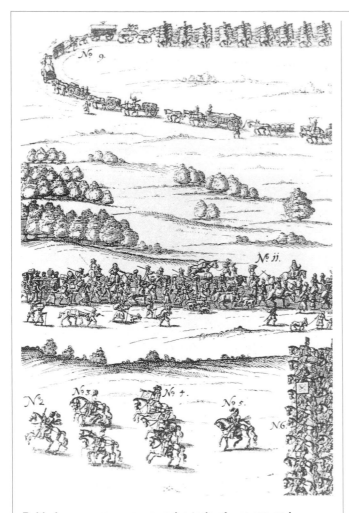

Behind every army was a massive train of wagons and baggage without which no army could function and Wallhausen quite properly included one in his illustrations. PEW.

farre'. While very light in comparison with traditional cast iron or brass guns, they were essentially one shot weapons, liable to burst if even slightly over charged or used more than once or twice. Although replaced in Swedish service in 1629 by lightweight all-metal 3lb 'regimental' cannons capable of repeated firing, the original leather gun concept had been brought to England in 1629 by Colonel Robert Scott. When he died in 1631, the concept continued to be developed by his nephew, Colonel James Wemyss, who was appointed master gunner of England in 1636. Siding with Parliament, he became Waller's Lieutenant-General of Ordnance in 1643, bringing with him a number of his leather guns. Captured at Cropredy Bridge in June with seven of his leather guns he returned to Scotland. Here he ironically provided Charles II's doomed army in 1651 with leather guns in time for its destruction at Worcester. Earlier, such guns had already found their way into the Royalist arsenal, two accompanying Wilmott's all cavalry force at Roundway Down in 1643. It should be stressed though that in none of these cases is there any record of the leather guns having any noteworthy role.

The Colours

Identifying regiments of foot, horse and dragoons on the battlefield was a common system of flags and guidons for each. For a regiment of foot, each company had its own colour, usually around 6.5 feet square and made of silk taffeta or sarsnet. Whilst details were often dependent upon a given colonel's whim, generally colours followed general rules of design. In *Animadversions of Warre* Ward observed that colonels 'ought to have all the Colours of his Regiment to be alike, both in colour and fashion to avoid confusion so that the souldiers may discerne their owne Regiment from the other Troopes;..'. Generally, all except the colour of the colonel's company bore a St. George's cross in the upper canton nearest the staff, occupying roughly one-sixth of the flag's field. The colonel's company normally had a completely plain flag in the colour of the rest, although there were a few examples of these bearing the heraldic badge of the respective commander. The rank of the respective company was indicated in a fairly standard fashion, the lieutenant-colonel's being plain with just the St. George's canton, the major's colour contained a wavy stream emanating from the St. George's canton known as a 'piles wavy'. The rest of the captain's colours, depending upon the seniority of the captain, had one or more of the particular regimental devices on the field. These devices ranged from roundels, stars, crosses, cinquefoils, crescents or even miniature versions of a colonel's heraldic symbol such as the dogs of Talbots regiment. Alternate systems existed. Charles Gerard's, Jacob Apsley's and the Duke of York's regiments all had the distinctive 'gyronnys' consisting of increasing numbers of coloured triangles to denote the respective company's ranking. Unique though were the colours of Prince Rupert's regiment, almost certainly designed by the Prince himself, consisting of various combinations of black, white and silver grey diagonal piles, the rank of each company being denoted by hollow black roundels. They were also unique in lacking the St.George's canton. Finally, artillery trains appear to have also had colours as a John Lott paid £11 in September 1642 for 4.75 ells (an English ell was 43 inches wide) of rich taffety for a colour for Essex's artillery train. It depicted two crossed cannons held in place by arms coming in from each side with an inscribed gold scroll at the top. It is possible that this colour was carried by de Bois' firelocks.

For both regiments of horse and dragoons, each

troop had a guidon, equally made of silk taffeta or sarsnet, roughly 2 feet square and fringed. At least for the horse, given that often each troop was the prerogative of its captain, a regiment's guidons often displayed great variation, particularly at the start of the war. Designs often had political or religious symbolism, though they were as likely to reflect the troop commander's heraldic sign. As the war progressed and individual troops became submerged in broader regimental identities, more standardisation emerged to reflect the respective colonel's preference. Given dragoons were essentially raised as regiments of foot, they carried cavalry guidons which tended to be miniature versions of infantry colours, although lacking the St. George's canton. Waller's dragoons for example had yellow guidons, with a number of black roundels depending upon the rank of the troop captain.

Scottish colours were generally similar to English, although obviously the St. Andrew's saltaire replaced the St. George and their Covenanter beliefs often ensured somewhat sombre and religious designs predominated. In 1639 it was recorded that all Scottish colours bore the motto, 'For Christ's Croun and Covenant', and in 1650 the Scottish Parliament ordered that all colours must bear the legend, 'Covenant for Religion King and Kingdomes'. Compared to England, there appears to have been a slightly greater use of armorial devices and sometimes actual numbers were used to denote the rank of the respective company.

Some of the most distinctive flags were those of the Irish where Roman Catholic symbolism predominated. During the summer of 1644 the Irish Catholic Confederacy dispatched a brigade of around 1,600 men under Alexander MacDonnell from troops raised in Ulster to support the Marquess of Montrose in Scotland. The 'True Informer' for 5th October detailed 12 flags. Examples ranged from a white field with a blood red crucifix and the motto 'aequum est pro Christo mori' (It is just to die for Christ), a blue field with the picture of Mary holding the infant Jesus in her arms and with her heels trampling on the serpent's head and the motto 'cunctas hareses

The hilt of a common soldier's pattern sword made by Jencks of Hounslow. The wooden grip has lost most of its original wire covering, although a tiny fragment remains at the foot of the grip. Gunnersbury Park Museum.

interemist' (Thou hast overcome all heresies), through to a silver/white field with a fully armoured knight depicted in the act of setting fire to John Calvin's book *Institutions* and the motto 'sic pereunt haresies' (So heresies shall perish). Other designs ranged through the crucifixtion, Jesus carrying the cross on his back, the Resurrection, variations on the Virgin Mary and even angels. Written mottos included 'in nomine Jesus omne genu flectitur' (In the name of Jesus every knee shall bow), and 'pro Deo, Rege and patina' (For God, the King and the chalice).

Soldiers' Clothing

By the 1630s, the clothes of a typical contemporary soldier were fairly standard throughout the British Isles. Despite popular perception, English, Scots and Irish soldiers were clothed in similar styles, albeit with a number of minor regional variations.

The Hat

There were essentially three types of common headwear, the Monmouth cap, the montero and the broad-brimmed felt, or beaver hat, metal helmets being reserved for battle. The former was undoubtedly the most common, 26,000 Monmouth caps being sent in 1641 and 1642 to the English troops in Ireland, manufactured at 23/-a dozen. Whilst there was no specific record of any being distributed before Edgehill, after Brentford a quantity of these hats were definitely issued from the Irish stores in London to Essex's men. Knitted from about 1lb of wool, then felted, Symonds wrote of their manufacture at Bewdley in 1644: 'The only manufacture of this town is making of caps called Monmouth caps, knitted by poor people for twopence apiece, ordinary ones sold for two shillings, three shillings, and four shillings. First they are knit, then they mill them, then block them, then they work with tassels, then they sheer them'.

When complete they had a moderately broad brim and probably had a leather hatband inside this to prevent the wool irritating the forehead. These warm and practical hats were undoubtedly popular with soldiers of both sides, with a common brimless variation to allow them to be worn under metal helmets.

Monteroes were equally popular, particularly with the Royalists, although there was no single variant of it. This hat probably originated in France earlier in the century and they generally resembled a jockey hat with two brims fore and aft. Some variants operated almost like a balaclava with a brim that could be pulled down around the face and back of the head. The ordinary soldiers versions were manufactured from wool cloth whilst officers versions were commonly made from velvet and decorated with lace.

The third type of headgear were the broad brimmed felt hats. There are no records of these having been issued to common soldiers, although they were certainly commonly worn by the gentry and officers. The superior versions were meant to be manufactured from beaver skin imported from North America, and even when not, were constructed from high quality felt. If heavily fulled and felted, the common soldier's Monmouth hat provided a cheap imitation.

The Suit of Clothes

While many soldiers began fighting in their civilian clothes, military clothes were issued to most at some point. These were commonly issued as suits and could include breeches, shirts, stockings and monteroes. Both coats and breeches were commonly made from dense wool broadcloth, the former lined either with a lighter weight wool or linen, the latter only with linen. Other materials used for coats were Kersey, a wool cloth described as 'a base and course kind of cloth for the use of poor people', and canvas. While there was no precise pattern for soldiers' coats, they closely reflected the straight cut style of the common labourer's coats, albeit with a number of more specifically military features. There appear to have been two broad variations, one with the outside made of two yards of Kersey, the other of one and one-third yards of Broadcloth. The key variation lay in the linings and fastening systems.

Thanks to the research of Stuart Peachey and Alan Turton, information for these come from two particularly detailed accounts of 7,400 suits provided by England for the Scots army in September 1644. Taking the totals of materials used to complete the order divided by the number produced, each suit used approximately 2 yards of broadcloth or an equivalent

This recreated musketeer's knapsack is just visible under his arm. English Heritage.

This recreated musketeer sports one version of the montero. English Heritage.

area of kersey, 2 yards of linen or lockram lining, a pair of leather pockets, 36 buttons and 6 pairs of hooks. A slightly less detailed return originated from Commissary George Wood in December 1645 for two options for 'magazine' suits. Wood can be seen as an experienced operator having been involved in earlier shipping clothes to Ireland. For the first option he listed for each suit 3.5 yards of northern kersey, 1.5 yards of lindsay cloth for lining the breeches and a pair of leather pockets. He set aside 1.5d for the tape binding the coat and for knee strings, and 1d for buttons and hooks for breeches, (a penny's worth of hooks, eyes and buttons could purchase 6 hooks and eyes and 6 buttons). For the second option he listed 4 yards of northern kersey or $2^{11}/_{32}$nd yards of broadcloth, 1.5 yards of lockram and a pair of leather pockets. He set aside 2d for the tape binding the coat, 2d for the knee strings and 1d for the hooks and buttons for the breeches.

Between the Scots coats and those of Wood there are several noticeable differences in terms of materials. Firstly, the number of buttons were reduced from 36 to about 6 and these were all specifically for the

breeches. These buttons could have been small white metal items or simply twisted pieces of cloth around a tiny piece of bone or the like. Secondly, there was sufficient lining material for the breeches but not the coat. Finally, while hooks were provided for the breeches, there do not appear to have been any eyes. Thus the Scots coats probably had 30 closely spaced small buttons down the front of the coat with the remaining 6 closing the fly on the breeches. In terms of pattern there was less variation, with apparently most coats made to a single size from one yard of cloth with a width of sixty inches. Coats were cut straight without a waist to reach down to just below the hip to minimise waste and complexity thus permitting rapid mass production by semi-skilled labour. Sleeves were long enough to be rolled back to reveal the lining, often with a small slit at the wrist to facilitate this. There was a short collar around one inch high and shoulder rolls or 'wings' where the sleeve entered the body of the coat. The latter appears to have been a specifically military feature. Finally there were normally two internal pockets in the lining, often made from leather.

In some references, 'cassocks' rather than coats were specified and it appears the terms were interchangeable. Technically the term cassock referred to a Dutch style of garment which could be converted from a coat to a cloak with buttons both down the sleeves and under the arms. Such garments were noticeably more voluminous and thus more expensive than a simple coat, requiring three or more yards of broadcloth for the outer layer and five to six yards for the lining. In addition, they required a considerable number of buttons, anything up to 180 if the sleeves, front, sides and rear were to be operated. Whilst such Dutch style cassocks were undoubtedly worn by officers, only specialist units such as the Earl of Essex's guard were issued with such.

The shorter doublets were also a common civilian item of wear many soldiers brought with them upon enrolment and a number were manufactured and issued as military coats. Made from wool or linen canvas and lined in linen, they commonly had six to eight hanging tabs. Although they cost around a quarter less than a coat, 6 shillings as opposed to between 8 to 11 shillings, their shorter length and narrower cut appears to have made them less favoured amongst the rank and file. Many portraits of officers show them wearing fashionable versions of this.

Whether part of a suit of clothes or issued separately, breeches were invariably made of broadcloth or kersey and lined with white or brown linen. Given the need to reduce costs, the common soldiers' versions were not particularly baggy, but rather loose fitting and generally cut to a universal length of around thirty-one and a half inches. They normally had tapestrings to tie them at the knee and a pair of leather pockets similar to those in the coat. The fly was normally closed by 6 buttons and around 6 pairs of hooks and/or eyes were sewn to the waistband to attach the breeches to the coat or doublet.

While a common item of wear for officers, waistcoats were occasionally issued to common soldiers. These were manufactured from almost anything that came to hand, wool cloth, linen and even old canvas or leather wall hangings. Generally these were very simply cut, being short and without sleeves, although they did occasionally have 4 hanging tabs in the style of the doublet with a short collar.

The shirts were commonly made from lockram or Osnaburg linen (linen could be made from hemp or flax) and cut generally from ten foot lengths between thirty-six and forty-two inches wide to essentially a single fit all size. With gussets added at the end of the neck, chest and thigh splits to resist tearing, the cuffs were simply gathered at the wrist with a small collar added to prevent the neck being chaffed by the woollen coat.

Stockings were made from either cotton or wool, the former being cut out, the latter being knitted or made from loosely woven woollen cloth. Generally white or grey in colour, woollen stockings could weigh as much as 9oz per pair

Footwear, Snapsacks and Buff-Coats

Possibly the single most important item for any soldier alongside his weapon was his shoes. For the infantry there were broadly two types, shoes proper and 'startups'. While many portraits of the wealthy illustrate a square-toed shoe with cutaway sides, this undoubtedly reflected a fashionable model. For the common soldier their shoes were round toed with closed sides made for strength rather than fashion, with a low heel. Made from the hides of bovine animals such as cows and ox, they were manufactured as straights, no right or left shoes in a pair, all were identical in shape. Mass produced in their thousands, particularly in Northampton and London, shoes had a life expectancy of three months during the campaign season. Soldiers of all armies would count themselves lucky if they received more than two pairs in any given year. As for startups, these were essentially calf-length boots which laced or buttoned up the front and were the common wear of rural agricultural workers. Whilst there are no records of startups being manufactured or issued to soldiers, it is certain many, particularly those forced to rely on their civilian cloths in default of military issue, wore these comfortable and practical items.

Heavy leather cavalry boots were popularly termed 'bucket tops', for although made to reach mid thigh, in practice they were rolled down to below the knee, thus resembling their familiar name. Although cavalry troopers were meant to be universally equipped with bucket top boots, shortages meant shoes were often worn in conjunction with leather, knee length gaiters called 'cockers'. These closely resembled later eighteenth century gaiters in design, buttoning up down the outside leg and extending over the top of the shoe.

The other major item of clothing made from leather was the buff-coat which was almost synonymous with the cavalry trooper. Originally developed as a padded fabric garment to give the

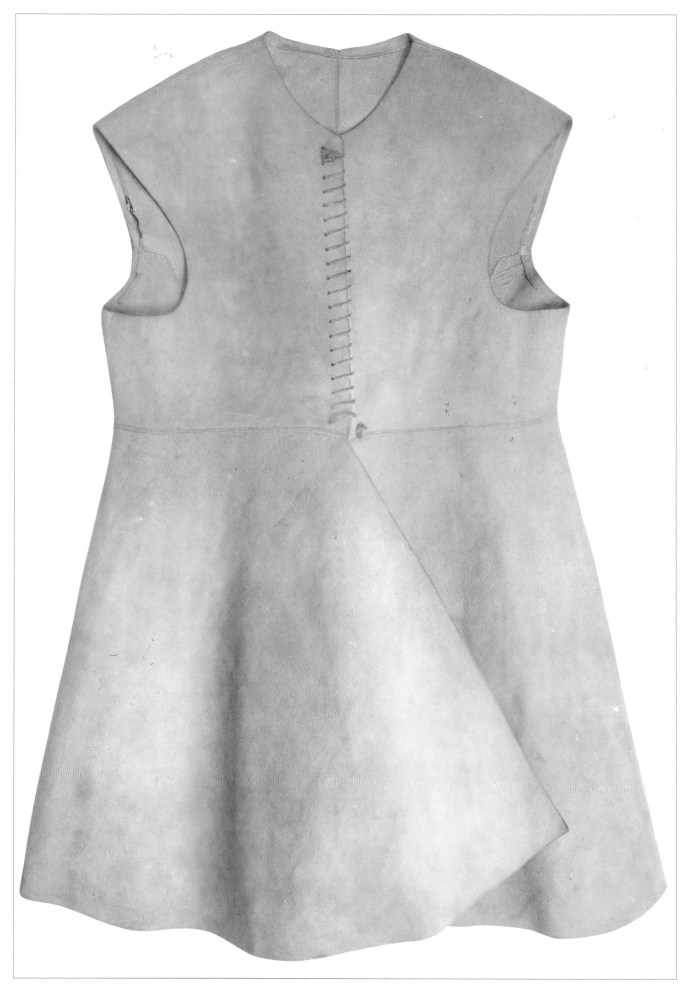

This recreated sergeant of musketeers snapsack is clearly in view as he prepares to give the order to give fire. English Heritage.

wearer an added layer of protection under their armour, by the early seventeenth century cloth had given way to leather. Although supposedly made from buffalo hide, the vast majority were manufactured from ox hide in shades ranging from grey/white through to bright yellow ochre reaching half way down the thigh. Whilst a true buff-coat was an expensive item mostly limited to officers, common troopers did receive cheaper versions. An individual officer might pay up to £10 for one which was fashionably cut and made from thick hide with a silk lining and metal clasps or silk strings to close it. Conversely, the troop of horse raised by the Liberty of Watford for Captain John Bird was issued with 53 buff coats and 52 pairs of leather gauntlets for a total cost of £100-9p whilst three troopers of Lieutenant-Colonel Thorpe's troop each received a buff-coat costing just 30/- each. These items would have been made from thin leather with no lining or decoration and simply closed by leather thongs down the front.

Finally, whilst not strictly speaking an item of clothing, most soldiers appear to have been supplied with a snapsack when issued clothing and shoes. Whilst variations in pattern existed, those issued to the military generally resembled a duffel bag style tube which was slung by a strap over the shoulder. These were normally made of canvas or leather and were substantial in proportions. Commonly, alongside personal items and food, a diligent soldier would carry a spare shirt, pair of shoes, stockings and other items of spare clothing in their snapsack. Soldiers of Essex's army in September 1643 each carried 3 days worth of provisions in theirs when marching to the relief of Gloucester, a weight in itself of between 4-9lb.

Uniform Colours

In respect of what colour coats and breeches were expected to be dyed, it appears red was already well established as the military colour for English troops. While Lawson demonstrated that there was some evidence for a preference for red coats and breeches during the latter part of the Elizabethan era, blue was equally popular. Certainly in the fighting against the Spanish in the Low Countries, the English soldiers under John Morris, Sir Philip Sidney, Lord Willoughby and Sir Francis Vere wore red cassocks. In 1585 the City of London equipped troops for service in the Low Countries in red coats and in 1590 troops

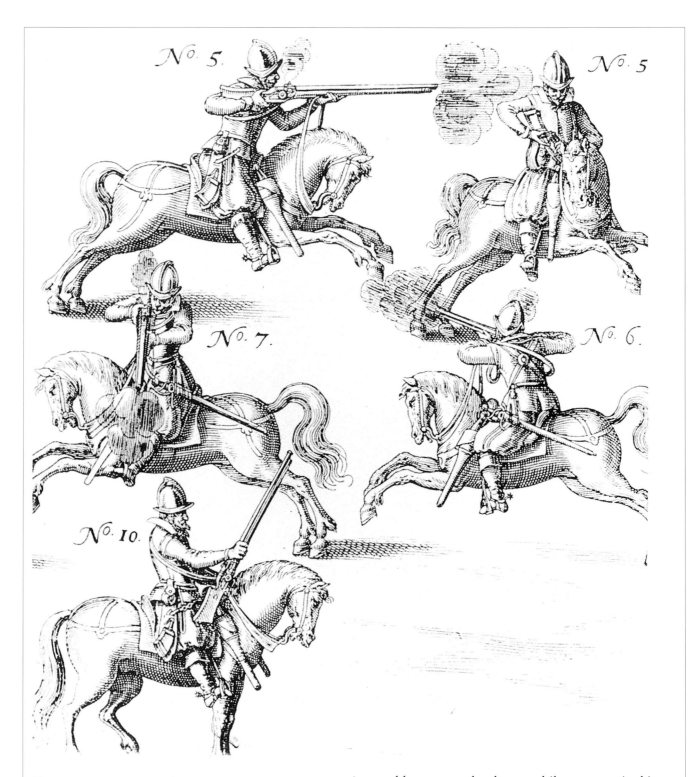

No. 5.

No. 5.

No. 7.

No. 6.

No. 10.

Almost all horsemen in the Civil War were equipped as harquebusiers. Here Wallhausen's illustration of 1616 ironically reflects how many Royalist and Parliamentarian horse would have appeared. Although buff coats had become fashionable, many horsemen would have considered themselves lucky to have been as well armed as these men, despite their lack of buff coats or back and breasts. The harquebusiers' 'port-flask' can clearly be seen on figures 5 and 10 hanging from their waist belts. PEW.

in Canterbury had their yellow coats changed to red. Yet in 1569 a corps of arquebusiers raised in Salisbury wore blue coats and red caps, whilst troops raised in Lancashire and Lancaster between 1576 and 1577 wore, 'a coat of blue Yorkshire broad cloth' and Yorkshire levies of 1587 had 'their cassocks and breeches of blue cloth...'. Having said this, by the eve of the First Bishop's War in 1638, red appears to have won out as the colour for soldiers coats as it was requested that, 'It would be good if Yr.Lordship's men had red breeches to their buff coats, because otherwise being country fellows they will not be so nearly habited as the other Lord's men'. Four years later as the Civil War itself erupted, although possibly referring to the coats of his own regiment, Denzill Holles' Sergeant Nehemiah Wharton on 13th September 1642 referred to, 'The countryman I clothed in a soldier's red coate'. Red continued to be favoured when available, being effectively institutionalised with the coming of the New Model Army in 1645/46.

Further support for the predominance of red comes from the recorded importation into Bristol between 1613 and 1655 of around 17,500lb of madder from Amsterdam per annum. As a single pound of madder could dye up to 10lb of wool red and an average soldier's coat weighed approximately 3lb, there was sufficient madder coming just into Bristol to dye 58,000 coats per year. Even deducting the use of some of this madder for civilian cloths, there was ample for military needs. Bristol also recorded an increasing importation of indigo from the West Indies for blue cloth, rising from just 224lb in 1613 to 11,816lb by 1655. When this is added to Somerset's own substantial production of native woad, then the predominance of blue for West Country regiments can be comprehended. Both red and blue could be obtained from a single dying process, as could a deep lemon yellow from the weed Weld or wold (luteola) and black using logwood. But the latter was expensive and very unlikely for the common soldier. Instead, a cheaper process using oak galls and green coperas (Ferrous Sulphate) could be used for bulk dyeing of black, but this was still more expensive than the former colours. Other than grey which was simply obtained by mixing black and white fleeces, all other colours required two or more processes and ingredients to achieve, thus making them more costly and less likely colours for soldiers' coats. Green was produced by first dyeing blue then yellow. Orange or tawney also required a double dyeing, first in red then yellow, the shade depending upon the proportions used. Purple could be attained by double dyeing with blue then red. Finally, white was possibly the most simple, either being undyed cloth or possibly bleached.

As stated, Scots and Irish soldiers were generally clad and equipped to an identical style and standard as their English counterparts, the 1,600 men of Montrose's Irish Brigade were all clothed and equipped as musketeers. Having said this, the Scots armies did have a number of distinctive elements to their clothing. Apart from the few Covenanter Scots regiments clothed by England in 1644 in red coats, all Scots soldiers, foot and horse, wore suits of 'hodden grey' wool broadcloth, an indeterminate shade of grey commonly worn by civilians. The lighter weight grey

wool kersey used for the coat linings was also utilised for stockings, although knitted stockings became common as the war progressed. While most soldiers wore the standard breeches of the era, some soldiers preferred trews, although again, these tended to be more noted amongst the officers than rank and file. Most distinctive though was the general issue of the blue Scots bonnet, an item of headgear favoured by both officers and soldiers and manufactured in the thousands. These were normally knitted and felted in a similar manner to Monmouth caps, although cheaper versions were cut from woollen cloth. The bonnets normally had a bunch of coloured ribbons attached to the left side to identify the regiment. Major Sir Thomas Hope of the Earl Lindsay's regiment noted on 8th January 1644, 'This day given to the soldiers of Craighall, who go under Captain Moffat, [ilk] of them their colours of blew and yellow silk ribbons'. Finally, the plaid was another characteristic feature of Scottish military attire, although these were not the voluminous versions popularly associated with highlanders, neither were they in 'clan' tartans. Rather they more closely resembled dull coloured blankets, around eight and a half by six foot serving both as a cloak by day and bedding by night. Inevitably, such distinctive clothes came to be worn by the Irish Brigade as it fought across Scotland.

Before leaving the Scots, there is evidence that the cloth used to make their shirts was rough to say the least. The Scots soldiers shirts were often made from 'harden', a particularly coarse type of linen. Due to particularly inclement weather, in 1640 Major-General Munro directed that in excess of 3,000 yards of harden be made into tents for his troops. Before this order was made up the weather improved and Munro had the harden made into shirts instead.

Officers and NCOs

Although commissioned officers were responsible for supplying their own clothes and equipment, this did not mean they simply wore civilian dress and styles. Obviously made of finer cloth and to far higher standards than any clothing issued to the rank and file, the styles of officers' clothes were unmistakably military, invariably adorned with silver or gold metallic lace. Colonel Jordan Prideaux reputedly wore a diamond buckle in his hat the day he was killed at Marston Moor whilst numerous contemporary portraits show well cut and laced buff coats were common. Further, for both Royalist and Parliamentarian officers, be they of the foot, dragoons or horse, red and scarlet appears to have been the favoured colour. Scarlet coat and breeches in particular appears to have been recognised as identifying professional soldiers, this shade having the additional advantage of being an expensive dye and thus reflective of sufficient social standing for an officers status. A contemporary account of a Royalist assault on Bradford by troops under Sir William Saville certainly twice identified officers by reference to 'scarlet' and 'buff' coats in respect of selecting targets. A reference to Lieutenant-Colonel Lilburne of Manchester's dragoons described him as 'drawing a paper book from under his short red coat' and a young dragoon officer of Tyldesley's, Captain William Blundell proudly described his red coat. This practice certainly included senior officers as a London newsheet of 1645 recorded Rupert as, 'clad in scarlet, very richly laid in silver lace'. This extended to the Scots and supposedly sober puritans. In 1644 Captain George Keith of the grey coated Earl Marischal's Regiment had a scarlet coat made for himself prior to marching into England, his mercer's bill giving an excellent illustration of a typical officer's apparel and its contemporary cost:

	£. s. d.
2 ells mixt Spanish cloth at 25s ye ell	02 10 00.
11 drop off silk (thread)	00 01 10.
2 Demibeaver hatts and tuo bands	02 04 00.
4 dison of silk buttons	00 01 00.
13 drop more silk	00 02 02.
1 pr pearle cullor silk stockings	01 10 00.
1 pr buckskin gloves	00 10 00.
9 yards silver and silk ribbons at 2s ye yard	00 18 00.
6 yards of changing satin ribbon at 10d ye ell	00 05 00.
4 ells of scarlit cloth at 20/ ye ell	04 00 00.
4 disane and ane half of gold and silver long-taild buttons at 14/ ye dosan is	03 03 00.
Suma is fyftein punds fyve shillings ster	15 05 00.

A similar bill must have been run up by the regicide Colonel Thomas Harrison who in December 1650 was recorded wearing a, 'scarlet coat and cloak both laden with gold and silver lace, and the coat so covered with clinquant, that scarcely could one discern the ground'. Obviously cultivating such display, this same Colonel Harrison had commanded the King's escort at his trial in January 1649 boasting, 'a velvet montero on his head, a new buff coat upon his back, and a crimson silk scarf about his waist, richly fringed'.

Apart from fine scarlet clothes, the two items of clothing which specifically identified a commissioned officer as such were his silk sash and gilt gorget, although the latter was apparently not always worn. The colour of an officer's sash usually indicated which

These four figures reflect the style of clothes common to officers of the trained bands. They were sketched from engravings on the brass clasps of the Great Vellum Book of the Honourable Artillery Company c.1635. They illustrate two commissioned officers at the top and an ensign and sergeant at the foot. PEW.

general they served under and while there were regional variations reflecting the preference of individual commanders, Royalists wore mostly red or crimson, whilst Parliament's were orange-tawny, the colour of the Earl of Essex. When Fairfax became Lord General of the New Model Army dark blue sashes replaced orange. Generally, these consisted of several yards of silk and if the many portraits of officers, particularly those by William Dobson of gentlemen in the King's Oxford Army, are to be taken as a reflection of general practice, they were often fringed and/or embroidered in metallic silver or gold thread. Officers' gorgets were equally highly decorative. These consisting of two plates which were pivoted on the left-hand side to enable the wearer to place it around their neck and was fastened on the right by means of a keyhole slot and mushroom-headed stud. While size and design was the prerogative of the individual officer, if contemporary

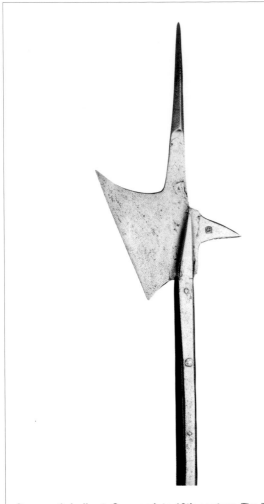

Sergeant's halbert, German late 16th century. The Trustees of the Wallace Collection, A952.

Book of the Honourable Artillery Company illustrates a sergeant in a particularly fine outfit. Caution though must be exercised in assuming all sergeants were equally as splendid as these examples. Wharton undoubtedly received financial assistance from his previous employer, the merchant George Willingham and the pre-war Honourable Artillery Company engravings illustrated well-to-do bourgeois merchants in ranks from private to captain, all dressed to their social rather than military station. Whilst dating from just after the war, another example of a well to do sergeant is in one of the stained glass panels from St.Chad's Church, Farndon in Cheshire of Sir Francis Gamul's yellow coated regiment. Here the rear view of the sergeant displays a fine embroidered buff leather baldrick supporting a sword over the right shoulder, a buff coat edged in lace set off by a fine laced shirt, gauntlet gloves and decorated breeches. As with the Honourable Artillery Company, Gamul's was a local trained band regiment from Chester indicating the likely presence of affluent officers and NCOs. Generally, unless in receipt of special funding, sergeants of field regiments wore cloths only slightly better than that of the ranks, albeit adorned with at least some metallic lace along with a sash and halberd to denote their rank.

Finally, paid and ranked as corporals were drummers and trumpeters who traditionally were provided distinctive clothing at the discretion of their colonel or captain. Both had to be mature and intelligent soldiers who knew both the appropriate drill and matching drum or trumpet calls to match. Reflecting both their distinctive role and the financial standing of their commander, drummers and trumpeters received clothing and equipment upon which much money had been lavished, bright colours, metallic lace and feathers often playing a significant part. The bill for the clothing of a trumpeter of General Brereton's troop included the following details:

> 2 yds of silver parchment at 1/2d per yd.
> 5 yds of fustian at 10d.
> 1 1/2 doz coat buttons at 10d each.
> 7 skeans of silk at 6d each.
> 1 yd cullered buckram 1/4d.
> 6ds of tape.
> 1 doz trussers 9d.
> 4 1/4 of 12d ribbon 4/3d.

portraits are to be taken as a reflection of general practice, gorgets were invariably engraved or chiselled with elaborate designs and decorated in gold or silver gilt inlay.

As for the junior, non-commissioned officers, corporals undoubtedly wore what was issued to the rank and file, there being no evidence for any special distinction for that rank. Sergeants though fell into a different category being essentially treated as what might be termed 'under' officers, or, as they were classified in the French army, 'bas' officers. They were distinguished by a silk sash, although probably not as embellished as some officers wore, and by the carrying of a halbert. In respect of clothes, it does appear they wore something better than that worn by those beneath them. There is Sergeant Nehemiah Wharton's description of 13th September 1642 relating that having received, 'my mistresses scarfe and Mr.Molloyne's hatband...had this day made me a soilder's sute for winter, edged with gold and silver lace'. Equally, an engraving from the Great Vellum

The Bishops' Wars and Ireland 1639-42

In describing how and with what English Civil War armies were clothed and equipped, it is easy to overlook where it originated. Many modern accounts ignore this element or make sweeping statements about imports from the Continent, and each sides access to weapons and equipment stored in Hull, the Tower, the County Trained Band arsenals and so on. While generally true for both sides at the commencement of the conflict, given the two to three months between the raising of the armies and the first major clash at Edgehill, there was in fact, an English armaments industry of some substance already in place well before the war began and it is from this and production facilities set up soon after the war broke out that much of the weaponry and equipment came from 1642 onwards.

Back at the turn of the century it was estimated by Sir Henry Lee that in the state armouries of the Tower, Westminster, Greenwich, Hampton Court, Windsor and the garrison forts there was sufficient armour to equip no less than 100,000 foot and 20,000 horse. Having said this, Sir Henry did not provide a breakdown of these blanket totals and it can be safely assumed that the vast bulk of it was of some antiquity and in various stages of decay. Due to the generally peaceful rule of James I, it was only in the early 1620s that a certain amount of modernisation was instituted with much of the old armour being sold off, some even being donated to the newly established colonies in Virginia and New England. In 1622, 500 to 600 plate coats, brigandines and jerkins of mail were dispatched to Virginia, although, according to the Commissioner of Ordnance, they were 'not only old and much decayed but with their age grown also altogether unfit and of no use for modern service'.

Under the new King Charles I, the mid-1620s witnessed three substantial military campaigns, the Count Mansfeld expedition of February 1625 which mobilised over 12,000 soldiers, the October 1625 Cadiz operation against Catholic Spain which mobilised 10,000 and the June 1627 Isle de Rhe expedition against Catholic France which mobilised over 8,000. Despite the abject failure of all three, they did occasion a degree of updating of English equipment as well as acting as a continued spur to efforts to improve the English militia. It was, however, the Bishops' Wars of 1639 and 1640 which acted as the first major stimuli to the English armaments industry in the seventeenth century , the King's armies requiring the production of large quantities of weapons and military equipment. When hostilities ceased and the English army in the north disbanded in early 1641, most of its equipment was taken into magazines established in Newcastle, York and Hull. With the outbreak of the Irish rebellion in October 1641, by early 1642 most of these stores were centralised at the Manor House in Hull to facilitate their being transported to London to replenish the stores at the Tower.

The Bishops' Wars

In the fourteen years before the Bishops' Wars the new King attempted to improve the country's only immediate source of armed men, the Trained Bands of each county. Whilst placing command in the hands of men of local position and influence helped ensure they had the ability to actually bring those enrolled out when called upon, it also ensured they generally had no previous military experience or knowledge. This meant that even if the local captain was diligent as to regular training sessions for his small body of men, these were often little more than opportunities for equipment and small arms drill followed by a social drink. Attempts at marching and manoeuvres often ended in confusion and were usually avoided. As to equipment, while they were meant to be equipped to the standard of regular soldiers, because the county had to pay for them there was no incentive to ensure either quality or modernity. Instead, weapons and equipment were purchased and maintained for as little

This well known woodcut of an English soldier in Ireland reflects important details of military fashion. The many buttoned coat has shoulder rolls/wings with tightly tapered sleeves rolled back at the cuff to reveal the lining. Partizan Press.

money as possible, with companies often sharing it by mustering on different days. Equally, there were no funds for clothing and the trained bandsmen simply wore their civilian attire.

Consequently, in the decades after the Armada scare and under King James's pacific rule, a great deal of inertia had set in amongst the Trained Bands to the degree that by the early 1620s many county forces were not being mustered together for even a token day's training once every three years. Equally, each county's magazine stocked equipment was both antiquated and often rusted and rotting. The only exception to this was in London where, as previously indicated, since the opening decade of the seventeenth century, social fashion for military issues ensured sufficient enthusiasm to achieve a degree of competence. Charles attempted to overcome these deficiencies, both through the issue of 'Instructions for Musters' and 'Directions', and by appointing professional soldiers as Muster Master Generals in

each county with the job of training and inspecting local companies. Generally though, whilst knowledge and understanding of the drill was marginally improved, neither this nor the state regulations did much to improve the quality of what was available in the county magazines by the outbreak of the First Bishops' War.

In November 1639, according to a report of arms issued: 'The foot arms were old, newly coloured, and mostly defective, though the rottenness of the leathers and buckles, and many so thin and slight as to be no way serviceable. The muskets have old barrels newly patched up and ill stocked, of divers bores wholly unserviceable. Some of the armourers averred that divers of the arms were known by their marks to have been issued out of the armoury some 15 or 16 years since. Many of the pikes were of fir-wood, with little old bodkin heads; others of ash, most of them sawn with broader heads, but not serviceable. The bandoleers, if worse may be, are worst of all. The musket rests are generally of fir-wood, and very short. Touching the horsemen's arms, we find the breasts by their heaviness to be part carbine, the rest pistol-proof. The back too light and thin for the heaviness of the breasts; we conjecture that some of them have been old backs to foot arms. The leathers rotten, buckles weak, pots very old, thin, and ill-fashioned as the back and breast. The pistols are too short, slightly wrought, of several bores, and we suspect will not endure proof.'

The army which was raised to fight the Scots was to prove less than wholeheartedly committed to the King's cause in terms of morale. Yet in terms of preparing the organisational ground work for the forthcoming conflict between King and Parliament, it proved far more effective than the previous decades

This woodcut of 1640 illustrates English soldiers destroying an altar rail and other 'Popish' objects on their march north to supposedly fight the Scots. The style of their dress suggests officers. PEW.

muster directives and in many ways provided a vital dry run for the conflict of 1642. It was directed that an army composed of 35,000 foot and 3,000 horse be assembled in Northern England. Whilst the King himself appointed the regimental colonels and signed the commissions of their subordinate officers, to provide the actual manpower each county was responsible for raising and clothing a set quota, although the Crown directly provided the arms and equipment.

Although many countys raised the numbers required, it could not be said that enthusiasm reigned. The Deputy-Lieutenants of Suffolk wrote to the council on 8th June 1640 that 'we shall do the best we can for the advancement of his Majesty's service in delivering the men to those appointed to receive them. The difficulty will be to make the number full, there being many run away. We have impressed the full number, coated and clothed them for service, and made hue and cries for those that have run away, and will deliver those that remain to Lieutenant Colonel Fielding'. Equally, the army's commander, the Earl of Northumberland wrote on 18th June that, 'I am advertised by the officers of Colonel Lundsford's regiment that of the 1,200 soldiers they were to have out of Somerset they have only 833'. Colonel Thomas Lunsford himself confirmed the problems of morale when he wrote four days later to Northumberland that, 'I find my regiment in the greatest disorder; divers of them in troops returned home; all are forward to disband and the countries rather inclined to foment their dislikes than assist in punishment or persuasions; hues and cries are of no effect,....[we] are daily assaulted by sometimes 500 of them together, have hurt and killed some in our own defence, and are

Woodcut of an English soldier in Ireland, although his desperate state of clothing would not necessarily have been unknown during the gruelling campaigns of the Civil War. Partizan Press.

driven to keep together on our guard. Notwithstanding we still march forward with as many as we can'.

Each county raised 'coat and conduct' money to pay for the clothing of each soldier and to escort them to the army. Reflecting the common lack of enthusiasm, some counties interpreted this literally and provided only a coat while others provided complete sets of clothing. These coats were, from the evidence, most probably in all cases uniform in colour. Certainly Sir William Savill's regiment in 1639 were recorded as redcoats and the city of Coventry bought 33 blue coats with linings at 15/- each and 24 blue breeches at 8/- a pair. Other purchases by the city included shirts, stockings, doublets, shoes and 1 yard of ribbon per man at 5d a yard. The state on the 30th of April ordered partizans (but not halberds) to be supplied with tassels 'the colour of each regiment'. That uniform coats were undoubtedley worn was confirmed by the entry in the Parish register of Carleton near Selby which recorded that 'William

Contemporary woodcut of 1640 illustrating the Treaty of Berwick portrays the musketeers as still equipped with musket rests and helmets, although the soldier on the far right apparently sports a wide brimmed hat. It is extremely doubtful any musketeer wore a helmet after 1641. PEW.

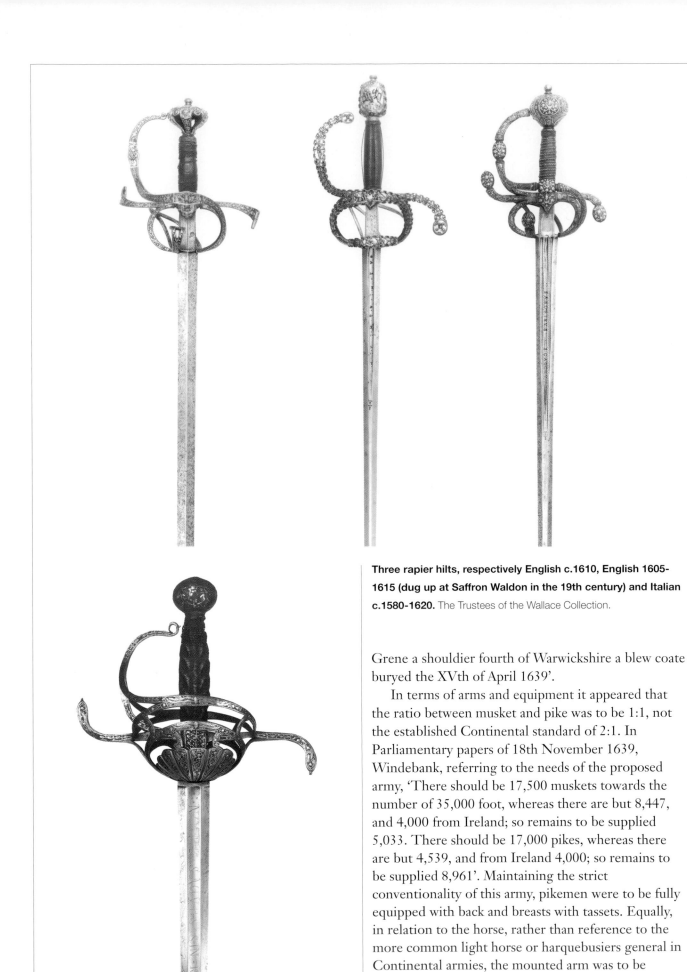

Three rapier hilts, respectively English c.1610, English 1605-1615 (dug up at Saffron Waldon in the 19th century) and Italian c.1580-1620. The Trustees of the Wallace Collection.

Grene a shouldier fourth of Warwickshire a blew coate buryed the XVth of April 1639'.

In terms of arms and equipment it appeared that the ratio between musket and pike was to be 1:1, not the established Continental standard of 2:1. In Parliamentary papers of 18th November 1639, Windebank, referring to the needs of the proposed army, 'There should be 17,500 muskets towards the number of 35,000 foot, whereas there are but 8,447, and 4,000 from Ireland; so remains to be supplied 5,033. There should be 17,000 pikes, whereas there are but 4,539, and from Ireland 4,000; so remains to be supplied 8,961'. Maintaining the strict conventionality of this army, pikemen were to be fully equipped with back and breasts with tassets. Equally, in relation to the horse, rather than reference to the more common light horse or harquebusiers general in Continental armies, the mounted arm was to be

English rapier sword hilt (with later blade) c.1625-30. The Trustees of the Wallace Collection, A641.

Closer side views of the guard of an English rapier. The Trustees of the Wallace Collection, A596.

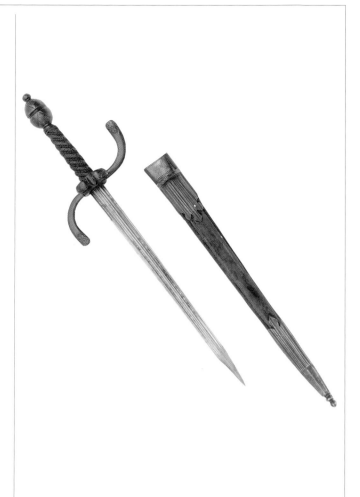

A left-handed dagger with original sheath (having provision for a by-knife), northern-European c.1610-20. These were still carried by some officers during the Civil War in addition to their rapier. The Trustees of the Wallace Collection, A783.

organised into 4 troop regiments of 508 'cuirassiers' and 'carabineers', to be drawn up in 25 files 4 ranks deep. Nonetheless, certain new innovations were present even at the start of the conflict with England's first full 600 strong regiment of dragoons raised in the north, including 200 from the Duke of Northumberland's own tenants and three full companies of firelocks to protect the artillery train.

Regardless of the rather antiquated ratios of musket to pike and the description of horse as cuirassiers and carabineers, English sources of manufacture required only ready money to make up many of the shortfalls identified by Windebank. On 16th December the gunsmiths of London, 'undertook to make for his Majesty 1,600 muskets a month, besides carbines and pistols...that 15,000 muskets be forthwith put in hand, whereof 5,000 to be of the larger size, or four feet in the barrel...and 10,000 of the shorter, or 3 1/2 feet'. Before the year was out they were able to petition the Lords and the Council of War that they had 'delivered into his Majesty's stores 3,502 muskets..., besides 1,057 pistols and 472 carbines'. As to costs, on 30th November John Watson

and others of the Gun-makers Company had undertook 'to supply monthly 1,200 muskets, 200 carbines, 120 pair of pistols, at the following prices: muskets, 18s.6d. each; firelock carbines, furnished, £1.16s. each; firelock pistols, furnished, £3. per pair; snaphaunce carbines, £1.2s. each, furnished; snaphaunce pistols, furnished, £2.5s. the pair'. Demand was such that by 8th June it was ordered 'That the Company of Gunmakers shall be hereby required to set in hand the making of 2,000 muskets a month, every musket to be four feet long'.

Other items were no less readily available, from John Gate and William Beauchamp, 'The price of bandoleers [for muskets], large size, well dressed ox-hide, with bullet-bag and priming-wire, 3s.each; next size, leather of same quality, 2s.6d. each. Fifteen hundred of these could be supplied for the first month from the receiving of our interest money, and two thousand each following month, so that we may have ready money'. From John Edwards and Robert Thacker, '..pike-makers. Can bring into his majesty's

A combed morion, Italian, 1590. These were going out of fashion by the 1630s. The Trustees of the Wallace Collection, A131.

A 'Spanish' morion, actually north Italian about 1580. These were termed 'Spanish' by the English, although they had no special link to Spain. This style continued to be fashionable amongst officers of the pike well into the seventeenth century The Trustees of the Wallace Collection, A137.

store monthly 400 long pikes at 4s.6d. each and also 500 musket-rests; white rests at 1s.1d. each, and black at 1s. each; provided we may have impress money and payment for goods on delivery and proof'. From Toby Berry, 'I am able to make 4,000 girdles, hangers, and belts monthly; the girdles and hangers at 2s., the belts at 1s.8d. apiece; provided I may receive £200 in hand, and the residue upon delivery of my goods'. The London armourers certified that they would be able to make 350 back and breasts a month and on 30th January 1640 it was ordered that a further 3,500 back and breasts, 21,000 swords and 2,520 pikes be produced from English sources. None the less, it proved necessary to seek yet further items from the Continent's well established military industries. On 24th January the Council of War directed the purchase of '7,000 muskets with bandoleers and rests in Flanders, and 2,520 corselets...also arms for horse, viz, for 500 cuirassiers and 1,500 carabineers'. On 30th April Sir Job Harby was issued a warrant 'to provide in Flanders or Holland 3,000 good pikes between 15 and 16 foot long..' as well as '3,000 muskets and 3,000 corslets..'. These overseas sources

were soon to be utilised by both sides in the forth-coming Civil War.

Ireland 1640-43

Given the general lack of commitment throughout England to conflict and the Scots military victory at the shambolic battle of Newburn, by the summer of 1640 the King had been obliged to accept the humiliating Treaty of Berwick. By November the Long Parliament was in being and the divisive political confrontation between Parliament and King had begun which would ultimately escalate eighteen months later into a military confrontation. Before this though, hardly had the army raised for the Bishops' Wars been reduced than Ireland exploded into revolt in late October 1641. On 1st November, Parliament received news of the rebellion and within 48 hours resolved 'that a drum shall be forthwith beaten for the calling in of volunteers'. After some debate, it was initially agreed that 6,000 foot and 2,000 horse were to

A 'Spanish' style morion helmet for an officer of pike late sixteen/early seventeenth century. Gunnersbury Park Museum.

Close-up of engraving on 'Spanish' morion helmet. Gunnersbury Park Museum.

be raised, although these totals were later increased to 10,000 foot. In addition, Scotland, with close ties to its newly planted Calvinist brethren in Ulster, also prepared to send upwards of 10,000 foot. Whilst there was little debate in Scotland over the question, that nation still being largely united in the aftermath of its victory in the Bishops' Wars, England was racked by division. Almost inevitably the raising of this army became caught up in the growing antagonism between the King and Parliament. The debate over who was to control this force played a significant part in triggering the final breakdown of relations. In fact, Parliament was to divert several of the regiments raised for Ireland to its own army to fight the King and just over a year later, the King was to recall a considerable proportion of this force to support his own cause. In many respects the army raised for Ireland in the opening months of 1642 merged almost seamlessly into preparations for the conflict in England.

Unlike the Bishops' Wars, the troops destined for Ireland were raised and equipped by the state, not the counties. Whilst there was mixed enthusiasm in England for the Irish army, Parliament rapidly succeeded in raising the 10,000 to 12,000 men asked for. These men came from two sources: a number of Protestant refugees already in Ireland but mostly volunteers from England. For the latter, many of those who had raised men for the counties in the Bishops' Wars now did so for Ireland. Resolving in November that 'one regiment shall be with all possible speed transported into Ireland under the command of some worthy person', Parliament appointed Sir Simon Harcourt to raise the first regiment. Within four weeks he had raised a full regiment of 1,100 men in Cheshire, being so successful that he had over 400 volunteers in excess and by 30th December Harcourt and his 1,500 men had landed in Dublin. Equally, the 1,500 strong, twelve company Lord Lieutenant's Regiment under Lieutenant-Colonel George Monck reached Chester for embarkation by 24th January along with Major Sir Richard Grenville's 300 horse of Philip Lord Lisle's regiment. Although a lack of shipping delayed their arrival in Dublin until late February, with other troops arriving, by the end of March over 3,000 foot and 400 firelocks had arrived.

Throughout the spring further troops poured in, including the regiments of Sir Michael Earnley, William Cromwell and Sir Fulks Huncks, mostly raised in Northern England. Whilst none of these colonels appear to have had any difficulty raising full regiments in excess of 1,000 men apiece, others were not so fortunate. Sir Charles Vavasour barely succeeded in raising 500 men from Devon and Cornwall, and the regiments of Lord Ranelagh, Sir William Ogle and Sir John Paulet equally fell short of their full establishments. None the less, ultimately nine regiments of foot, a regiment of horse and two companies of dragoons were raised and dispatched from England. In addition, a number of regiments were raised in Ireland. There were already thirty-nine companies of foot and fourteen troops of horse in the Old Standing Army in Ireland when the rebellion erupted. By the summer of 1642 this had risen to eight regiments of foot, thirty three troops of horse and a train of artillery. With the addition of the privately raised 'Adventurers' force, paid for by a group of London merchants, by August 1642 in excess of 40,000 English and Irish troops had been raised and equipped.

To provide these troops with arms and equipment, the records still survive of the initial series of warrants issued, between 6th November 1641 and 18th February 1642, alongside the arms issued and waiting in the arsenals to meet the demands. Confirming the standard ratio of two muskets to one pike, a total of 8,948 muskets, rests and bandoliers, and 3,982 pikes were warranted for. This was sufficient to arm all nine regiments of English Foot and three Irish regiments, the Lord President of Munster, Sir John Clotworthy and Lord Conway's regiments. There were also warrants for 50 partizans, 106 halberds and 101 drums. To arm and equip Lisle's regiment of horse and the ten troops, warrants for 1,723 carbines, 1,483 pairs of pistols, 6,866 swords and belts, and 2,038 saddles were issued. It should be noted that the swords were for both the horse and pike, such weapons not being considered necessary for the musket. Whilst the types of swords were not differentiated in these orders, a later list of 20th September 1642 for 8,000 swords divides them equally into basket hilt swords for the horse and long rapiers for the foot, both supplied with belts. Finally, 324 dragoon muskets were warranted for the three troops of such.

Interestingly, no warrants were apparently issued for or other mention made of armour, either for pike or horse. Neither appears to have received the 'back, breasts and pots' which were still conventionally identified as appropriate for such troops. While it may just be that the records for the armour have not survived, it is likely they were not considered priority items for service in Ireland. As would become the practice a decade later, the nature of the theatre of war in Ireland already dictated adaptations in equipment.

In respect of clothes, because of the turmoil in Ireland little could be sourced there and the troops initially arrived wearing mostly their civilian attire. Rather, the full range of garments, including coats, breeches, waistcoats, shirts, stockings, and large probably brimmed Monmouth Caps, were supplied directly from England, although local labour was available to finish some items, snapsacks being sent out as kits. Not only did this inevitably cause delays leading to complaints that 'Many of them [soldiers]....fall sick daily through cold for want of clothes and shoes', when supplies did arrive, clothing was generally of poor quality, some being simply unserviceable. When, in July 1642, 3,000 coats arrived from England it was complained that 'the cloth is bad and the coats too short and scant and want lining and we have no doublets or breeches to be issued with them'. The generally dismal quality was further emphasised by the description of the Lords Justices of 6,000 suits and caps which finally arrived in September, the 'cloth is very bad, the suits ill and slightly made up, the cassocks not lined, the lining of the breeches very bad cloth, the caps so little as they cannot be useful for the soldiers and such of them as were brought to this board are so little as they can hardly come on the head of a child'. To add insult to injury the prices charged were described as 'very wild, excessive and unreasonable'. Of greatest concern and giving rise to the greatest number of complaints was not the poor state of the common soldiers' clothes but shoes 'their want of shoes exceeds [clothes] and is general, without which they are neither able to march nor do any service at all'.

The major reason for these failings was corruption. One supplier, John Davies, an Irishman and friend of Sir John Clotworthy, was appointed as commissary for the despatch of goods. Utilising the traditional arts of bribery and corporate entertainment he was able to charge 18s.0d. per yard of cloth which would normally, given the material was very coarse and shrinkable, have sold for at most 8s.0d. Equally, cassocks and breeches for which he charged 17s. 0d. could be purchased for 10s.0d. Consequently, although initially allocated £4,000, Davies was able, within nine months, to obtain over £12,000 from Parliament. In an attempt to deal with this and improve quality, the Lord Justices in Ireland drew up a list of what each soldier should be provided with by

The fact this re-enactment soldier has a tent to cook before possibly means he belongs to the artillery train. English

their captain. Each soldier was to receive a good suit of clothes, two shirts, three pairs of stockings, three pairs of shoes and a hat. The phrase, 'a suit of clothes' was becoming a commonly used term which became the norm in the forthcoming English Civil War as a convenient method of describing the coat and breeches which were to be supplied as a uniform set along with various hats, shirts, stockings and knapsacks as circumstances permitted. As would equally become familiar to future generations of soldiers, they paid weekly deductions from their pay of 10s. for these clothes. Parliament was also concerned at the spiralling costs, poor quality and irregular deliveries to Ireland. Against the background of preparations for fighting the King, in September 1642, Parliament directed that each soldier should be provided with a cap, canvas doublet, cassock, breeches, two pair of stockings, two pair of shoes and two shirts. Each set of clothes was to cost 42s.6d. with again each soldier's

pay being deducted each week. Although problems of quality were never overcome, quantity had been addressed, as by June 1643 Parliament had placed various orders to supply troops in Ireland amounting to 18,000 coats, 15,000 breeches and 23,000 pairs of shoes.

Ultimately, the army in Ireland remained poorly maintained, due in no small part to the outbreak of the English Civil War and that conflict's priority in terms of expenditure. Poorly maintained and fragmented across the provinces of Ireland, this army did well to defend the Protestant cause until the 'Cessation' in 1643. Nonetheless, the effort of providing clothes and equipment for this vast force on the very eve of the English Civil War had two divergent impacts. Whilst it denuded many of the Crown's arsenals that fell into Parliaments hands, it conversely ensured that the double impact of the Bishop's Wars and the Irish rebellion had stimulated the industries providing military equipment, particularly in and around London, thus priming them to meet the demands of the coming conflict.

The Parliamentarian Army 1642-46

Parliament's First Army

With the deterioration of relations between King and Parliament to the point when Charles had fled London in late January 1642, Parliament's thoughts turned towards securing military support. Having only partially succeeded in attempting to seize control of the nation's trained bands with the Militia Ordnance in March, by July it was felt necessary to raise their own army. Whilst Parliament was to ultimately raise numerous armies as well as provide assistance to their Scottish allies from 1644 onwards, the balance of surviving material means this chapter deliberately focuses primarily on the main field armies of the Earl of Essex and the New Model Army.

Parliament's possession of London meant that they were able to divert the preparations being made for Ireland directly into the new army which was to be raised by the Earl of Essex as well as a reserve army under the Earl of Warwick. In the spring of 1642, five further regiments had been authorised for dispatch to Ireland, Lord Wharton's, Lord Kerry's, Charles Essex's, Thomas Ballard's and William Bamfield's. In the event only Lord Kerry's departed under its Lieutenant-Colonel, William St.Leger, the remaining four being transferred in July to form the cadre of the twenty regiments of foot authorised by Parliament for Essex's main field army.

Having designated the sixteen colonels for the balance of the twenty regiments, on Thursday 28th July, volunteers from London and Southwark began to be registered at the New Artillery Gardens. On 1st August these volunteers began to be divided into companies for the first three regiments, Holles', Chomlies' and Merrick's with company officers being appointed at the same time. Once sufficient men had been embodied, regiments departed London at various times during late August and early September, Essex assembling ten regiments of foot at Coventry on 19th September, the Earl of Essex's, Denzil Holles', Sir Henry Chomlies', John Hampdon's, Earl of Stamford's, Lord Robart's, Earl of Peterborough's, Lord Oliver St.John's, Lord Wharton's and Lord Rochford's. Four further regiments were directed on Oxford, namely Lord Brook's, Thomas Grantham's, Sir William Constable's and Sir William Fairfax's. By early October, with the arrival of Sir John Merrick's, Lord Saye and Seles, Lord Mandevile's, Charles Essex's and Thomas Ballard's, Essex had assembled a force of nineteen adequately armed, equipped and uniformed regiments of foot in the south west Midlands. Given the time scale, supply and logistical difficulties, this was no small achievement.

Joining them were 42 troops of horse, raised across the south-east and east Anglia. Each troop was generally raised by individual members of the gentry, one such being a Captain Cromwell, although it is doubtful his troop actually arrived in time for Edgehill. Totalling just over 2,000 men, most of these disparate troops were divided into eight regiments of horse, although defective staff work ensured some troops remained as independent bodies. The eight regiments were, The Lord General's (under Sir Philip Stapleton), the Earl of Bedford's, Sir William Balfour's, Lord Feilding's, Lord Willoughby of Parham's, Sir William Waller's, Edwin Sandy's and Arthur Goodwin's. The rather adhoc nature of Parliament's horse went some way towards explaining their poor performance at the commencement of the war. Finally, an artillery train of some 46 guns was assembled under the none too effective direction of Lieutenant-General of the Ordnance Philibert Emanuel de Boys. As with the infantry, much of its equipment was drawn from existing preparations made for Ireland and the substantial stocks in the Tower.

Back on 6th August, to provide clothes for the infantry, the Committee of Lords and Commons for the safety of the Kingdom had ordered that all 'the soldiers shall have delivered unto them at their first marching coats, shoes, shirts and caps, in all to the value of 17/- for every man; and Stephen Eastwick and

The recreated musket and pike of the Fairfax Battalia prepare to march. English Heritage.

Captain Player are requested to provide all such as are yet unprovided by the Irish committee'. Listed on the reverse of this document to receive this were all twenty of Essex's regiments of infantry, of which only William Bamfield's failed to ever join him. This equipment was received from the Irish stores on 19th August and issued to each soldier as a standard set of coat, pair of shoes and a snapsack on the 22nd. The first regiments to be equipped were Holles, which received 809 coats and 1,200 pairs of shoes and snapsacks, Chomlies', receiving 521 coats and 1,200 pairs of shoes and snapsacks and finally Merrick's, which received no coats, but 492 pairs of shoes and 1,200 snapsacks. Equally, between 15th August and 6th September, Eastwick acknowledged receipt from the stores of the Irish Adventuers of 1,200 shirts, 267 pairs of shoes, 450 snapsacks and 4,368 shirts. Whilst most other regiments were raised in London, Colonel John Hampden's regiment was raised shortly thereafter in Buckinghamshire and it was not until 17th September that it received 1,000 sets of coat, shoes and snapsacks. Whether from stores already assembled for Ireland, or items newly ordered and manufactured, throughout August and September, in fact up to the very eve of the battle Edgehill, Essex's regiments continued to receive clothes and equipment in the field. In addition, each regiment received £80 for their 'coulors, partizane, halberts and drums'. Whilst some regiments were undoubtedly equipped in London before departure, others initially marched in their civilian clothes, receiving clothes and equipment on the march. The warrants issued for this process unquestionably demonstrate that regiments were clothed in coats of a uniform colour and generally equipped to a standard pattern, although they also imply soldiers had to rely on their own devices for headgear.

The Earl of Essex's were warranted to receive in excess of 1,740 coats, being mostly of orange although upwards of 240 were tawney, the latter possibly for its company of firelocks. It was also warranted to receive 1,500 shoes, shirts and snapsaks. Colonel Denzil Holles were warranted to receive 1,200 coats, shoes and snapsacks, the former being red. Warrants were issued for Colonels Sir Henry Chomlies', Sir John Merrick's and Lord Stamford's regiments to each respectively receive 1,200 coats, shoes and snapsacks, the latter in addition to receive 1,200 shirts. Chomlies' and Stamford's were blue coats whilst Merrick's were described as the 'London Greycoats'. Colonel John Hampden's were warranted to receive 1,400 coats, shirts, shoes and snapsacks, at least 400 of the coats being green. Lord Robart's were warranted to receive 935 sets of coats, shoes, snapsacks, the coats being red. Lord Wharton's, Lord Rochford's, Lord Mandeville's, Lord Peterborough's, Lord Oliver St.John's, Colonel Thomas Grantham's, Colonel Sir William Constable's, Colonel Sir William Fairfax's and Colonel Charles Essex's were each respectively warranted to receive 800 sets of coat, shirt, shoes and snapsacks. In addition to these standard sets of clothes, Mandeville's, Constable's and Essex's were warranted to receive 800 'caps', although these were ultimately not received. As for recorded coat colours, Rochford's and Constable's were blue, Grantham's and Essex's tawney, Peterborough's red and Fairfax's grey. Lord Saye and Seles was warranted to receive 871 sets of coat, shirt, shoes and snapsacks, Lord Brook's 740 sets, the former being blue coats, the latter purple. Finally, Colonel Thomas Ballard's were warranted to receive 837 sets of coats, caps, shirts and snapsacks, its coats being grey. As with other regiments allocation of caps, they failed to arrive prior to Edgehill.

Unlike the survival of warrants for the government issue to the infantry in the Public Records Office, apart from the issue of tawny-orange silk sashes in 1642 at the rather extravagant cost of 10s. each, there was no mention of any clothing being supplied for Essex's troops of horse. The reason was essentially a social one in that for the horse, raised by the gentry, each captain was personally responsible for the provision of clothing and equipment to his troopers, traditionally his own tenants, whilst they were generally still responsible to supply their own horse. The monies were then reclaimed from the government. Whilst many troopers were generally recruited from outside a given landowners estates, the feudal traditions prevailed and company and regimental commanders retained responsibility. What evidence exists though indicates that, as with the infantry, there were recognised set standards, each trooper receiving a coat, shirt, stockings, boots and spurs alongside their obligatory armour. In addition, whilst again there is no surviving evidence of the general issue of such items, buff coats were considered common wear as were cloaks to keep off the rain. For example, the Earl of Bedford as Lord Lieutenant of Devonshire requested in 1642 that the county horse should 'be handsomely furnished' in 'comely apparrell, with coat of buff with long skirts' and a 'coat of clothe to keep both himself and furniture from the violence of the weather'. Having said this, there is little

evidence that buff-coats were common item for Parliament's men even after Edgehill as there are no surviving records indicating the supply of any such item to any units of Parliamentary horse.

As for the colour of the uniform items, grey was apparently preferred for coats and cloaks, whilst certainly red or scarlet breeches had been popular in the Bishops' Wars. Having said this, there were red cloaks and grey breeches. Whitlock commented upon meeting Mr.Francis Russell of Essex's Lifeguard that he had 'twelve of his servants in scarlet cloaks well horsed and armed'. Equally, although from later in the conflict, in May 1644 the quartermaster of Captain Roper's troop of the Earl of Denbigh's Horse (this regiment had been Lord Fielding's at Edgehill) was issued eight and a half yards of grey cloth.

The Earl of Warwick's reserve army of seven regiments of foot equally received clothes, albeit a little after Essex's. During November and December Colonel Philip Skippon's regiment of foot received a staggering total of 2,310 coats, shirts and snapsacks, but only 1,500 shoes, the coats being red lined yellow. Colonel John Holmstead's received 1,200 coats, shirts, shoes and snapsacks, the coats being red lined white, whilst Colonel George Langham's received at least 1,356 coats, shirts, shoes and snapsack, its coats being blue lined white.

In terms of arming and equipping the respective armies at the outset, the advantages would appear to have lain firmly with Parliament. Yet, while Parliament held the main arsenals of the Kingdom: the Tower, Greenwich and Woolwich, Kingston-upon-Thames, Portsmouth and Hull, in fact, few of these state arsenals were satisfactorily stocked on the eve of the Civil War. The demands of the Bishops' Wars, the Irish Rebellion and Parliament's own interference with powder manufacture, all combined to leave many of the arsenals almost empty, except Hull which contained sufficient arms for almost 16,000 infantry and 2,000 horse, assembled for dispatch to Ireland. In contrast, by April 1642, the Tower held only 1,367 muskets and 354 pikes, while in July 1642 the Earl of Essex was looking to arm the 20,000 infantry, 4,500 horse and 500 dragoons Parliament had commissioned to be raised. With a standard ratio of 2:1 musket to pike, 13,400 muskets and bandoleers were required for the shot, whilst 6,600 pikes, swords, back and breasts, and helmets were required for the pike. Equally, the horse, as harquebusiers, required swords, carbines, pistols, corslets, helmets and saddles, although the dragoons could manage with standard infantry equipment, requiring only saddles for their mounts. Most of this came from Hull, from whence, from May onwards, 7,238 muskets, 1,658 pikes, 3,729 swords, 2,295 cavalry carbines, 49 brass pieces of ordnance and much miscellaneous material was transported to London by sea. Even when added to what was in the Tower, Essex faced a significant shortage of basic equipment for the infantry with few bandoleers for the shot and little or no armour for the pike. For the horse the shortages were far greater. There was no cavalry equipment at all in the Tower and although Hull supplied ample swords, carbines and pistols, there were only 160 back and breasts, and 210 helmets available by July.

In the meantime, the Lieutenant-General of the Ordnance at the Tower, the Royalist Sir John Heydon, had been continuing preparations for supplying the army in Ireland. Having asked the various armourers of the City of London for a report of their stocks and the rate of supply of new equipment, they responded on 13th April. The Guild of armourers was able to supply from stock 300 sets of harquebusier, 60 sets of cuirassier armour and 500 foot arms within two weeks. The Pike makers could supply from stocks 500 pikes and rests respectively and manufacture similar quantities each month. The Bandoleer makers had immediate stocks of 2,000 and could produce between 2,000 and 2,500 per month. The Cutler's could offer from stocks 1,200 pikes, 3,000 swords, 300 halberts and 100 partizans. Finally, the Girdle makers could provide from stocks 3,000 sword belts and 1,000 carbine girdles, and could produce per month 5,000 and 2,000 respectively.

The departure shortly thereafter of most of the senior officers of the Ordnance to join the King in the North, including Heydon and William Legge, the Master of the Armouries, left matters in considerable confusion until Parliament appointed its own officers. Owen Rowe and John Bradley, both London merchants and officers of the trained bands, were given the task of acquiring new arms and armour from the various suppliers in the city as well as abroad. Orders were placed in France and Holland to purchase 12,000 muskets with rests, 1,200 carbines, 6,000 pikes, 6,000 back and breast, 1,500 pistols and 600 harquebuses [carbines]. By early October, 5,580 pikes, 2,690 muskets, 3,956 rests, 2,331 back and breasts, 980 pair of pistols, 246 carbines, 66 dragoons and 401 harquebuses had arrived from the continent and been issued to the army.

In a way, it was fortuitous that the numbers initially raised for Parliament fell short of expectations, particularly in terms of the horse. In the event, Hull and the Tower provided sufficient weapons to field all of Essex's 13,000 or so men at Edgehill in October as well as Warwick's reserve army, although most pike and horse appear to have been without armour, and many musketeers without bandoleers. For example, whilst Lord Wharton's regiment were warranted to receive 500 muskets with bandoleers and rests, 500 belts and 500 back and breasts, Saye and Seles were warranted to receive just 300 muskets and 200 pikes. Whilst none of Essex's soldiers were unarmed, they were certainly not equipped to the highest standard, nor did his regiments of foot necessarily field the standard ratio of 2:1 in terms of shot to pike.

Parliament's War Effort

The equipping of Essex's army places into perspective just how crucial the retention of Hull was to Parliament when Sir John Hotham twice refused the King entry during the political manoeuvring immediately prior to the war. Without the weapons stored at Hull, Parliament could only have equipped its field army by stripping the London Trained Bands of their equipment. Yet only a few weeks after Edgehill, it was these trained bands who played the key role in blocking the King at Turnham Green, a

This well equipped musketeer wears the common Monmouth cap and straight cut soldier's coat common to many of Essex's army. Partizan Press.

This contemporary woodcut depicts various civil disturbances which occurred in London during the summer of 1643. The soldiers in both pictures are undoubtedly members of the London Trained Bands. In the top picture Popish images were being burnt and the soldiers appear to be wearing fashionable open kneed breeches and straight cut coats. In both, all but one figure (the ensign in the top left hand side), the headgear was the broad brimmed hat. PEW.

pivotal action which was only possible due to the retention of their weapons and equipment. In fact, as the war progressed it was levies of the London Trained Bands which made up significant shortfalls in the infantry manpower of both Essex's field army during the crucial September campaign of 1643 and Waller's re-built army which defeated Hopton at Cheriton in March 1644.

In fact, many accounts of the war hold that for Parliament, their sources of supply and production were excellent from the start, holding as they did the major arsenals of England as well as the east and south. In fine deterministic logic, they then identify why Parliament won the war, given their apparent superiority in resources. It is very true that England's

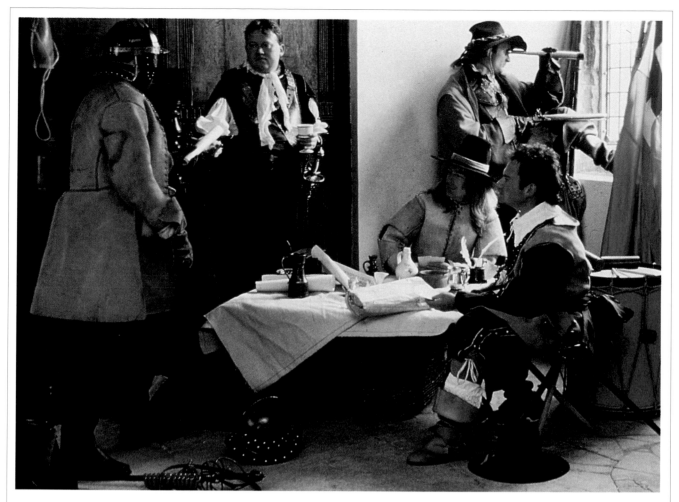

A group of re-enactment officers discuss tactics whilst another watches through a spy glass for the enemy. English

armaments industry, which was based on iron, was centred in the ancient iron producing region of the Weald in Surrey, Sussex and Kent which also had easy communication with the Tower. Around the Tower itself, many gunmakers set-up shop in the Minories, setting-up the London Gun Company in 1638 to exploit their near monopoly. As the warrants issued during the Bishops' Wars revealed, the London workshops could manufacture upwards of 1,600 muskets per month. Despite this, Parliament faced many difficulties: they were dependent upon the King's Gunfounder, Brown, who, while he was tied to the iron mines and woods of the Weald and to the Tower which took most of his output, was essentially a royalist at heart and very lukewarm in fulfilling Parliament's orders. This was also reflected in the major Hounslow sword-maker Jencks who left, with most of his workmen for Oxford even before Edgehill. Further, Parliament's powder-mills and stocks of gunpowder were seriously run down and Parliament was initially denied the vital commodity of coal with Royalist control of Newcastle, the shortage of which seriously interrupted the production of firearms in London until mid-1643. Hence, although not reliant on imported weapons and munitions from France and the Low Countries, Parliament required such sources to make up the difference between domestic production and the constant demands of the battlefield. Consequently, the control of sea-ports was of considerable strategic importance and goes some way to explain the number laid siege to by both sides. Parliament obviously began with an enormous advantage given its hold on London, Bristol, Plymouth, Hull, Dover and Portsmouth along with the navy. Although Bristol fell to the King in July 1643 and both Plymouth and Hull were effectively cut off for much of the war by Royalist siege lines, there was never any effective interruption to the receipt of imported materials.

Finally, at the beginning of the war, the organisation of Parliament's arms supply was rather amateurish: of the nine pre-war principal Ordnance and Armoury officials at the Tower, six remained loyal to the King and joined him (a higher proportion than in the royal civil service generally). Hence, the Committee of Safety was obliged to fill their places with an army paymaster and the appointment of a gentleman described as 'late Citizen and hosier of London'.

80 The Parliamentarian Army 1642-46

Opposite.

Given the three piles wavy on the colour carried by this ensign of the recreated Fairfax Battalia, it probably belongs to a senior captain. English Heritage.

Essex's Field Army 1643-45

For Essex's army, after the initial clashes at Edgehill and Brentford, the winter and spring of 1643 saw its depleted ranks re-organised and re-enforced. Over the winter and spring nine under strength regiments were reduced, Holles', Brook's, Fairfax's, Wharton's, Mandeville's, Grantham's, Charles Essex's, Rochford's and Peterborough's. To counterbalance this, on 22nd November the seven regiments of the Earl of Warwick's reserve army were incorporated into Essex's army, Philip Skippon's, James Holbourn's, Henry Barcley's, John Holmstead's, George Langham's, Henry Bulstrode's and Anthony Stapley's. Having been joined by an infantry brigade from the Eastern Association in the spring, he successfully captured Reading in April. His army though was now decimated by disease, probably typhus. Given that at this point the Royalist supply situation was improving, the irony here was that this epidemic was partially due to a failure by Parliament to issue any fresh clothes despite its undoubted resources enabling it to do so. Between 11th April and 21st June, Essex's regiments each lost an average of five men per day, Skippon's 376 out of 1,033, Langham's 360 out of 908 and Robart's 330 out of 723. With fears for the fall of Gloucester, drastic measures were required if Essex was to be able to march to its relief, particularly as by early August, Essex was describing his men as 'most almost naked'. Rigorous petitioning of Parliament plus a rapidly deteriorating military situation forced, on 10th August, 'the house (to) conclude for the clothing of your army, the which clothees will be speedily sent'. This ordinance directed the supply to the army camped north of London of 'coats, shirts, shoes and snapsacks to the number of 10,000 of each sort..'. Whilst most of the coats, shoes and snapsacks arrived between 25th and 30th August, other items did not and given the desperate needs of all his regiments this partial delivery caused Essex to complain that there was 'sent to the army a proportion of shirts, shoes, coats and snapsacks which are so unevenly provided that I know not how to dispose of them without a damage to the army by a mutiny, there being no stockings and so few shirts'. In the event, to avoid trouble, only those items, coats, shoes and snapsacks of which there were sufficient quantities to supply all regiments were issued, the insufficient batches of shirts remaining in wagons.

In terms of equipment the situation appears to have been more stable. At the Tower, by the end of March 1643 Bradley and Rowe had purchased 19,513 bandoleers (over half being of tin-plate), 261 drums, 21,189 swords, 599 back and breast, and at least 6,346 muskets. It ought to be noted that throughout the war there was not a single warrant, either for the manufacture of or issue of helmets to the pikemen of Essex's regiments. It may be safely assumed therefore most wore a variety of the soft headwear. Equally, there were few if any musket rests issued after 1642 and it is most likely that those which existed rapidly found their way into a camp fire as useless encumbrances. The new muskets being manufactured were becoming lighter, sometimes being termed 'bastard' muskets, the average barrel length decreasing from four to around three feet with corresponding savings in the weight of the wooden stocks.

The re-issue of coats often meant a change of coat colour, there not being the luxury of matching those

Colonel Edward Aldrich's blue colours with gold laurels were made up in December 1644 whilst still part of the Earl of Essex's forces, they were carried though by his next regiment in the New Model Army. Partizan Press.

Given the impedimenta behind him, this recreated buff coated officer might well be responsible for the guns of the garrison.
English Heritage.

previously issued. Whereas the majority of coats issued in 1642 were red, shortages meant many were grey in 1643. A letter to Skippon apologising for the shortages in a batch of coats, blaming a lack of linen and wool in London, went on to list the coat colours of those included:

> Red linned Red 520.
> Red linned White 220.
> Grey linned Red 540.
> Grey linned Yellow 500.
> Grey linned White 560.

In addition, a report on the army in Mercuricus Rusticus for November commented, 'for now country grey begins to be parliament grey', suggesting a noticeable predominance of that colour.

To ensure Essex was strong enough to relieve Gloucester he received various re-enforcements, some of whom were uniformed. A brigade of the London Trained Bands joined him, consisting of two regular units, the Red and Blue regiments, and the Blue, Red

and Orange Auxiliaries. Despite these London regiments being described by colours, this referred, as it always did, to their flags, not their coat colours. In fact, whilst well equipped, like most trained bands those of London marched and fought in their civilian clothes. Also from London were Colonel Randall Mainwaring's regular regiment who had been clothed by the Committee of Safety in red coats. Finally there were two Kent regiments, Sir William Brook's and Sir William Springate's, for whom no recorded clothes issue survives for 1643, although in February 1644 Springate's were issued red coats. It was therefore a predominately red and grey coated army which Essex led to relieve Gloucester and fight the King at the First Battle of Newbury during September.

The winter of 1643/44 saw sickness and desertion again devastate the ranks of Essex's foot, the average strength of each regiment dropping to around 120 men. With the aid of the London Trained Bands and other local regiments, Essex was able to counter Royalist pressure around Newport Pagnell. As per the previous spring, to re-build his foot Essex disbanded the three weakest regiments, Langham's, Constable's and Holmstead's, detaching two others to garrison duties, Ballard's and Thompson's. To fill the ranks of the remaining eight regiments of foot, the flow of volunteers having dried up, conscription was resorted to for the first time. There does not appear to have been any re-issue of clothes prior to Essex's men joining with Waller's army in early June. Consequently many of the new conscripts must have campaigned in their civilian clothes whilst the remaining veterans must have made do with the tattered issue of the previous year. The standard of clothing, particularly footwear, cannot have improved as these regiments marched, first after the King's field army in company with Waller and then swinging into the West Country during July. By the time these foot soldiers came to abject surrender at Lostwithiel in August their clothing must have been far from uniform or even decent as they were stripped and forced to trail back to Portsmouth.

While many writers have suggested that the soldier's red coat only became normal attire with the coming of the New Model Army, in fact there is little doubt that for Parliament's forces red had already become the predominant coat colour. Although Essex's soldiers had received significant batches of grey coats in both 1643 and spring 1644, the disaster which overtook it in Cornwall ironically ensured its return to red coats. In the aftermath of the Lostwithiel debacle in August 1644, all of Essex's 6,000 foot had to be fully rearmed, equipped and clothed. On 7th September

Parliament directed that, 'six thousand foot arms, and five hundred pair of pistols and six thousand suits of clothes, shirts etc...' be rapidly dispatched to Portsmouth where Essex's stripped soldiers had assembled. Ironically, this was the first time since the war had commenced that all these soldiers, as opposed to just a proportion, had been issued clothes from head to foot. As early as 21st September 2,000 suits and 3,000 arms were delivered to Portsmouth and throughout September various convoys of clothes and equipment arrived, including suits of clothes, shirts, stockings, shoes, snapsacks, bandoleers, muskets, drums, partizans, halberts and so on. Much of the clothing appears to have come from Edward Harris who was to be contracted the following year to supply coats and breeches to the new Model Army. All the

This somewhat speculative series of figures illustrates the changing cut of soldiers' uniform suits during the Civil War. On the left wearing a montero is a soldier in a fashionably cut civilian doublet with breeches tied at the knees. For the central figure the demands of war have seen a tighter, more economical cut to his coat and he wears a brimless Monmouth cap. Having said this, his breeches reflect the current fashion for being open at the knee. The right hand figure may represent the clothes made up for the New Model Army, his coat being closed by laces down the front rather than buttons. Partizan Press.

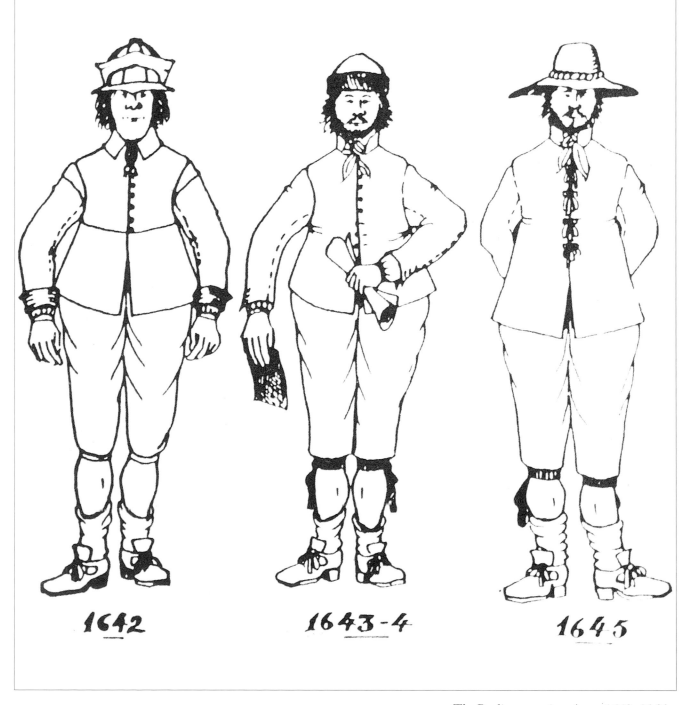

1642　　　　1643-4　　　　1645

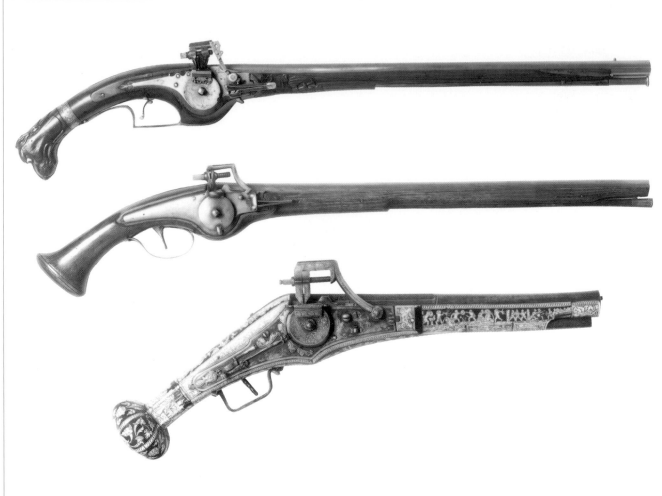

Three pistols: (bottom) German wheel-lock 'puffer', (top) Dutch c.1640-50 and (middle) French c.1640. The Trustees of the Wallace Collection.

evidence suggests that the predominant coat colour was red. The Weekly Account for 15th January 1645, in reporting Rupert's abortive attempt on the 11th to storm Abingdon, held by Essex's men, referred to the, 'brave garrison...and of my Lord Generals Army whose Red coates did now as gallently as at Newbury...'.

In terms of equipment it appears the experience of war had brought major changes to Essex's army. There was apparently a marked increase in the ratio of musket to pike, 6 muskets being issued for every pike and these muskets were becoming lighter as the use of musket rests had long ceased. Equally the pikemen seem to have completely abandon the use of armour. In fact, since early 1643, there had been no orders at all for the manufacture of pikeman's back and breast's and none was delivered to Essex's men after Lostwithiel. Swords though were now universal, sufficient being delivered for all infantry to receive one.

A bandoleer of the type used by the New Model Army. The Board of Trustees of the Royal Armouries.

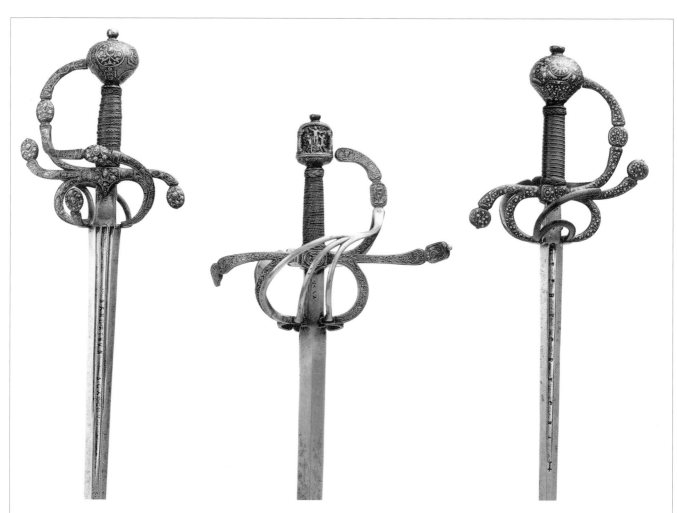

Three sword hilts: composite (left) German and two English, c.1605-15. The Trustees of the Wallace Collection.

The New Model Army, 1645-1646

It is fortunate that the almost complete set of contracts survive for the New Model Army from its inception in April 1645 to almost the end of the war in March 1646. The volumes containing the contracts were almost lost in the early 1800s when the Ordnance Office in the Tower threw out these notebooks as 'waste paper'. Fortunately they were saved before being destroyed by a Benjamin Nicholson and are today available in the British Library.

The evidence the contracts for the New Model Army offer as to the clothes and equipment of the New Model Army clearly demonstrated the impact of three years of warfare. Firstly though an old error needs to be put to rest. There are three sets of contracts for coats/cassacks and breeches which have been held up to prove that all the foot of the New Model Army wore red from the army's inception in

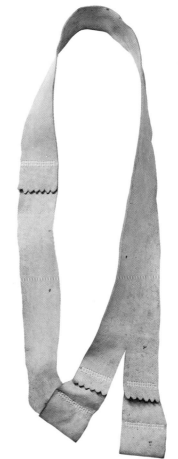

A baldrick of buff-leather from Littlecote House. The Board of Trustees of the Royal Armouries.

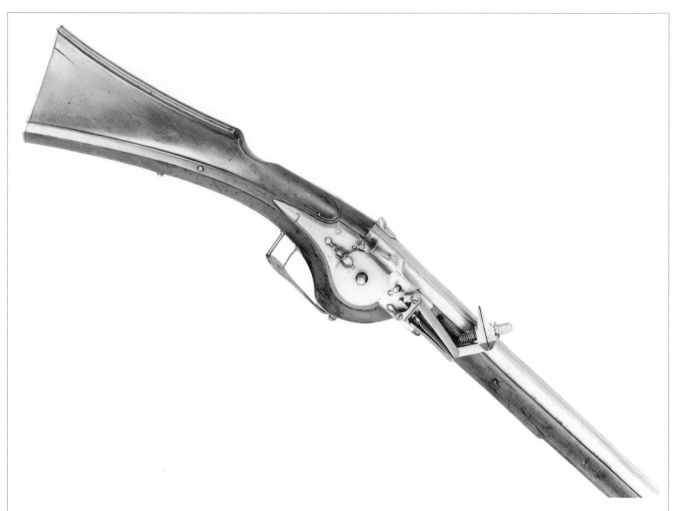

Detail of the butt-end stock, including lock and part of the barrel of a French plain 'military style' wheel-lock c.1620 from the cabinet d'armes of Louis XIII, King of France. This type of firing mechanism was still common amongst harquebusiers. The Trustees of the Wallace Collection, A1111.

April 1645. As the first of these orders was not placed until August 1645 with the other two in February and March 1646 (dated to the old calendar as 1645), then prior to September 1645 it would seem the New Model Army fought in the clothes each regiment had worn when in Essex's, Waller's and Manchester's armies respectively. Having said this, there is considerable evidence to suggest most of the foot already wore red, those delivered later to the New Model Army simply maintaining an already established practice. Further, as men were impressed in London, East Anglia and the south east to fill its ranks in the spring of 1645, the respective counties were instructed to clothe them before dispatch to the army, the county of Essex doing so in 'red coats faced with blue'.

Equally, as the clothes and equipment specifically contracted for the New Model Army were not delivered until late 1645, there was irrefutable evidence that red was already the predominant colour,

not just of Essex's infantry but of Manchester's and Waller's too. This came in a report in Perfect Passages for 1st May 1645 of the completed New Model Army marching out from Windsor towards Oxford, 'The manner of Sir Thomas Fairfaxes march is thus...Major Generall Skippon marched in the van of the foot and leadeth the Generalls own regiment; Sir Thomas Fairfaxes Colours are blew; the men are Red-coats all the whole army, only are distinguished by the several facings of their coats, the fire-lockes (only) some of them are tauny coates; and thus the regiments of foot march one after the other'.

Although saying little in respect of the army at Naseby, what the contracts for the New Model Army do reveal is precisely how and with what a 'model' army of the late war was equipped, given warrants

Opposite.

Top.

A musketeer's powder flask of flattened cow horn, Flemish, dated 1594. The Trustees of the Wallace Collection, A1261.

Bottom.

The musketeer's powder flask viewed from the reverse to display the belt-hook and fittings. The Trustees of the Wallace Collection, A1261.

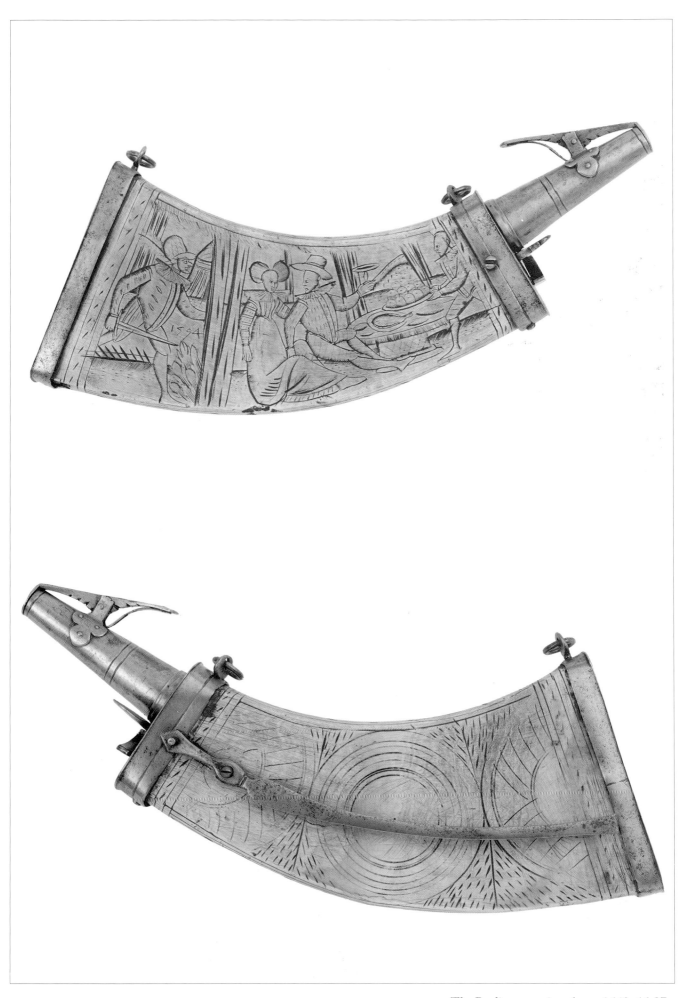

88 The Parliamentarian Army 1642-46

Helmet for an officer of pike c.1630, probably Flemish. The Trustees of the Wallace Collection, A88.

were ultimately issued to re-equip each and every soldier, be they foot, horse, dragoon or gunner.

In all respects the New Model Army was just that, a model Dutch army. Assembled in April 1645, the infantry had an establishment of twelve regiments totalling 14,400 men. The three existing armies totalled less than half that figure, Essex's mustering 3,048, Manchester's 3,578 and Waller's just 548. This required the impressment of 8,460 men. Ironically its model nature meant it reverted to the ratio of 2:1 in terms of musketeers to pikemen. The establishment of the cavalry was equally text book, with regiments from Essex's, Manchester's and Waller's armies being combined into eleven regiments of horse. Unlike the infantry though there was no significant shortfall in the ranks and the veteran New Model's cavalry were undoubtedly Fairfax's elite force, particularly the six regiments originating from the Eastern Association

Opposite.

This recreated New Model Army firelock reflects the style of clothes from towards the end of the Civil War, particularly in respect of his open knee breeches. English Heritage.

including Cromwell's near legendary 'Ironsides'. Finally there was a single 1,200 strong dragoon regiment under Colonel Okey, again the combination of the dragoon regiments of each of the three pre-existing armies, alongside an artillery train including two companies of firelocks.

In clothing, equipping and arming this army, almost for the first time in English history, the novel idea of standardisation was introduced. It was required that manufacturers had to provide set patterns of their products which they were held to match in mass production and to deliver to the Tower of London for inspection. Consequently many of the contracts specified remarkable detail for whatever the item may have been and also demonstrated how London had developed what can only be described as a varied and substantial military industry capable of rapidly delivering both quantity and quality. From mid 1645 through to 1646 the totals delivered were remarkable, 8,050 matchlock muskets, 3,300 firelock muskets, 5,600 pikes, 10,200 coats/cassocks, 9,000 shirts, 20,200 snapsacks and 23,700 pairs of shoes. Commencing with the New Model's legendary uniform red coats and other uniform clothing, an example was that of 14th February 1645/46 with Richard Downs of London:

A fine officer's buff-coat, gorget, sash and sword. English Heritage.

'Two Thousand Coates and Two Thousand Breeches at seventeen shillings a Coat & Breeches

'Two Thousand paire of stockins at Thirteene pence halfe penny a paire.

'The coates to be of a Red Colour and of Suffolke, Coventry or Gloucester-shire Cloth and to be made Three quarters & a nayle long (29.25 inches) faced with bayse or Cotton with tapestrings according to a patttern delivered into ye said Committee.

'The Breeches to be of Grey or some other good Coloure & made of Reading Cloth or other Cloth in length Three quarters one eight well lined and Trimmed sutable to ye patternes presented, the said Cloth both of ye Coates and of ye Breeches to be first shrunke in Cold water.

'The stockins to be of good Welsh Cotton.

'That although it is impossible for any person to undertake to make ye sayd provisions exactly suitable for goodness to any patterne for yt many wil be better and some may be a little worse yet it is ye resolution of ye said Contractor and he does hereby promis that as neere as he can none of ye said provisions of Coates, Breeches & Stockins shall be worse than ye patternes presented to ye said honorable Comittee'.

A contract for 3rd August 1645 was similar in that they were in batches of two thousand, although here the reference was to 'cassacks and breeches' along with shoes. There was though no suggestion that the use of the term cassack as opposed to coat was anything else but the written style of the author.

The contracts for March 1645/46 were slightly different again; the totals were the same: two batches of two thousand from Richard Downes, the first two thousand in a week, the second two thousand in a fortnight, the colour of the 'tapes' however was very varied, 'ye tape to bee white, blew, greene, & yellow...orange'.

An example of one of the numerous orders for shoes was that of 5th January 1645/46, 'There Contracted wth Jenkin Ellis of Katheren Tower for 4,500 payre of shooes neate leather wth good soles of the sevrall sizes of Tennes, Eleavens, Twelves and thirteenes of each size a like number all of them to be punched & each payre tacked together & marked on the soles wth the severall markes hereafter mentioned at 11s 11d a payre to be brought into the Tower of London to be viewed wthin one moneth...'.

Shirts were to be of 'good Lockram' and 'Snapsacks large & of good leather'.

Over 9,000 infantry swords and belts were ordered, an example being that of 3rd August 1645, 'Contract wth Robert Gilbert and Richard Rumsey for 1000 swords and belts....Dutch blades'.

Also ordered from a variety of suppliers were 'matchlock...muskett English full borc & proofe', and '...Pikes of good Ash sixteen foote long wth steele heads at three shillings Xd a pike...'.

All musketeers were supplied with bandoleers, over 24,000 being contracted for, an example being, 'The Boxes of the said 2000 Bandileers to bee of wood wth whole Bottoms to bee turned wthin and not bored, the Heade to bee of wood and to bee layd in oyle, vizt Three times over and to bee coloured blew wth blew and white strings, wth strong thred twist and wth good belts att XXd a peece to bee brought into the Tower of London, and to bee received imediately,...'.

Not all the bandoleers were manufactured from wood as 4,000 were of either iron or copper plate and unusually all were from one supplier, suggesting specialist skills, as on 7th January 1645/46, 'There contracted wth Thomas Jupe, Thomas Roch & Nathaniell Humfreys of Michaells Crooked Lane for 4000 Bandeleers the boxes of strong double plate the heads the same wth whipcord string & with good Belts according to the patterne at 20d apeece to be brought into the Tower of London'.

What might be termed the miscellaneous items of drums, colours, halberts and partisans were ordered from specialising suppliers of such. The following order, although amongst the papers of the New Model Army was dated 16th December 1644 and referred to Colonel Edward Aldriche's new colours which were produced as a result of the Parliamentary defeat at Lostwithiel. When Essex's army was integrated into the New Model Army, Aldriche took his new colours with him.

'There is due unt Alexander Vener Ensigne Maker ye summe of Eighteene pounds To be pd out of such moneys as Remayne in ye hands of Sr Walter Erle Knt Lieutenent gen. of ye Ordnce Recd by him at Habberdashers hall for ye buying of Drums, Ensignes, partizans & Halberts for ye Lord Generalls Army (By Order from ye Comons House of Parlyamt dat 28 Nov 1644) ffor ye buying Drums, Cullers, Halberts & partizans for ye furnishing of Collonell Aldrich his

Top.
'Pappenheimer' style rapier hilt, gilded overall, northern European c.1630. The Trustees of the Wallace Collection, A645.

Bottom.
A two-piece gorget for wear over a buff coat, German or French c.1640. The Trustees of the Wallace Collection, A237.

Cromwell's Ironsides at Naseby, 14 June 1645.

Cromwell's illustrious Ironsides were the epitome of Civil War troopers, yet despite popular misconceptions, the horse of both sides were indistinguishable in terms of equipment and appearance, being mostly harquebusiers. In the plate opposite, Cromwell's troopers brush up against Royalist pike at Naseby. The iron pots and corselets provided the primary protection from edged weapons, although the heavy buff coats were almost as capable of turning a blow. Equally, whilst the heavy leather boots are turned-up to give the rider the best grip possible, they also provided considerable protection from blows to the legs. Here, given the situation, the nearest trooper has chosen to discharge one of his pair of flintlock pistols, leaving his sword sheathed. The flintlock carbine suspended from a buff leather shoulder belt was primarily for picket and outpost work. In the background is an officer, identifiable by his sash and a Zischagge helmet with plume.
Painting by Christa Hook.

Regimt. vizt ffor VII new Ensignes made of blew florence sarsnett wth Distinctions of gold culler Laurells wth tassells to yem'.

The equipment and arms ordered for the horse reflected the ideal for harquebusiers, with the exception of buff-coats, there not being a single mention of such, either in the warrants or for items issued. Equally, whilst the dragoons were supplied with saddles these were very basic affairs compared to those of the horse, costing less than half the price. For example, on 5th June 1645 an order was placed with one of the major supplies of mounted furniture, Elizabeth Betts, '...for one hundred and fourty Dragoone new saddles with furniture at Seaven shillings and siz pence p saddle....One hundred Troope sadles with furniture & stran-bitts at Sixteene shillings and sixpence p saddle'.

In terms of weapons the horse were fully armed with firelock carbines, pistols and swords. On 10th January 1645/46 it was, 'Contracted wth William Burton of the Minories for 59 Carbines full bore & [pro]ofe wth Swivells at XIIs IXd a peece to be forthwith brought into the Tower of London'. On 22nd December 1645, 'agreed wth William Gardner of the Minories & Godfrey Pety of the Minories aforesaid for two hundred payre of snaphaunce pistolls full bore & [pro]ofe with holsters of Calveskins inside & outside well sewed & liquored at XXs IIIId a payre to be brought into the Tower of London'.

As for cavalry equipment, examples were those of 10th January 1645/46, 'Contracted wth Henry Thrale of Algate for 820 Carbine belts of good leather & strong buckles according to the patterne at 8d a peece & for 500 Cartridge Girdles at 2s 8d a dosen to be forthwith brought into the Tower of London'. On 26th June 1645, 'Contracted wth Sylvester Keene for 200 backs brests and potts English at XXs p suite'. On 2nd July 1645, 'Contracted with Mr.Edward Barker for Two hundred potts with three barres English at VIIs a peece'. On 3rd April 1645, 'Swords & Belts-3200-The Mr Wardens & Company of Cutlers in London att 5s per sword & belt whereof 200 horsemens swords'.

The regiment of dragoons, whilst clothed as per the infantry, were armed and equipped according to their specialist role. All dragoons were armed with short firelock muskets, an example being that of 10th January, 'Contracted with John Silke senr of white chappel for Two hundred snaphaunce Dragoones full bore & [pro]ofe at 12s 4d a peece to be forthwith brought into the Tower of London'.

Uniquely it appears they were also equipped with early cartridge boxes as on the same day it was, 'Then Contracted wth Nathaniell Humfreys of Michaells Crooked Lane for 1200 Cartridges the boxes of strong plate covered wth black leather 700 of them halfe round & the other 500 double at Xd a peece..'.

Finally, amongst the vast array of other items required by a seventeenth century artillery train, horse harness, gunners and engineers tools, guns, mortars and the like, there were orders for tents, 'Tents for the Trayne 200 of John Snow Tentmaker the Tents VIIen foote long VIIen foote broad and six foote high of good Lockeram according to the pattern & wth firre staves, lynes & pinns & other appurtenances according to ye best Trench Tents at XXs p Tent'. None though were ordered for either the infantry or horse who were still expected to make do with hedges, barns and the habitats of the long suffering local populace

Thus as the English Civil War finally drew to a close, the soldiers of Parliament's New Model Army were finally able to take the surrender of the few remaining Royalist garrisons, fully equipped to the most modern of standards. Its infantry and dragoons were universally clothed in red coats, grey breeches and well shod, each regiment with its distinctive coat lining colour displayed at the cuff. Whilst its shot and pike were fully armed to the established 2:1 ratio, there was apparently no armour, be it back and breasts or helmets, worn by the latter. Equally, the horse were well armed and although armour does appear to have remained a key item of equipment there was still no evidence of them receiving clothing or buff-coats.

The Royal Army 1642-46

An Army Fit for a King, Edgehill 1642

Having been disappointed in his expectations of the trained bands and refused entry to Hull, the King only began to seriously raise troops in July 1642. Utilising a feudal prerogative power, he issued commissions of array to various supporters to raise regiments of both foot and horse. By September the Royalists proved generally successful at raising the manpower for a substantial field army in Wales, the north east, north west, and parts of the West Country. The problem proved to be providing these men with sufficient weapons and equipment. Given the availability of information on Royalist clothing and equipment, the bulk of this chapter concentrates upon those regiments serving directly under the King's command which became known as the 'Oxford Army'.

What the well equipped Royalist soldier should have had would seem to be beyond doubt as a summarised version of the idealised picture contained in the 1638 *Directions for Muster*, was distributed in the King's *Military Orders and Articles*:

'The Arms of a Pike-man, are, Gorget, Curats, head-piece, Sword, Girdle, and Hangers.'

'The Arms of a Musquetier, are, Musquet, a Rest, Bandeliers, Head-piece, Sword, Girdle, and Hangers.

'It is required, that the Musquets be all of a Bore, the Pikes of a length.'

These Articles added details for the equipping of the horse, reflecting in respect of the first category the still prevalent ideal of the cuirassier and a degree of confusion over the distinction between the light horse and dragoons in that: 'The Armes of Horsemen, Cuirassiers, are, a Gorget, Curats, Cutases, Pouldrons, Vmbraces, a left hand Gauntlet, Taces, Cuisses, a Cask, a Sword, Girdle and Hangers, a case of Pistolls, Firelocks, Saddle, Bridle, Bit, Peterell, Crooper, with the leathers, belonging to fasten his Pistolls, and his necessary sack of carriage, and a good horse to Mount.

'The Armes of a Hargobier or Dragon, which hath succeeded in the place of Light-horsemen (and are indeed of singular use almost in all actions of War) the Armes are a good Hargobus, or Dragon, fitted with an Iron work, to be carryed in a Belt, a Belt with a Flaske, Priming-Box, Key, and Bullet-bag, an open Head-peece, with cheecks, a good Buff-coat with deep skirts, Sword, Girdle, and Hangers, a Saddle, Bridle, Bit, Peterell, Crooper, with straps for his Sack of necessaries, and Horse of lesse force and lesse price than the Cuirassier'.

In reality these were at best aspirations as the King faced considerable difficulties in providing even the basic weapons mentioned. A clear sign that the King had an early appreciation that he would face shortages was the dispatch of the Queen to Holland on 23rd February 1642 in an attempt to pawn the Crown Jewels to raise money for arms. Having said this, one of Charles' few early advantages was that the senior Ordnance and Armoury officials, particularly the highly competent Sir John Heydon, remained loyal. Having managed to scrape together a respectable if rather ragged artillery train of 20 guns in time for Edgehill, these officials enabled the establishment of an efficient Ordnance department in Oxford once that city became the King's headquarters in late October. In the months preceding the first major clash of arms at Edgehill, having issued the first Commissions of Array in July without an equivalent source to Hull, he was reliant initially on militia stores and private arsenals. Inevitably, the quality of equipment from these sources was varied to say the least although having said this, sufficient equipment was found to equip an army of 12,000 men who were more than able to hold their own against Parliament's forces.

The King began to concentrate his army somewhat later than Essex, raising the Royal Standard in Nottingham on 22nd August. By the time he departed Nottingham on 13th September there were only some five weak regiments of foot: Sir William Pennyman's, Sir Ralph Dutton's, John Belasyse's, the King's Lifeguard and the Lord General's. In addition, he had

Side view of a German (Nuremburg) burgonet c.1600. The Trustees of the Wallace Collection, A99.

assembled between 500 and 800 horse in a number of independent troops and 12 guns. Given its location closer to the Royalist heartland in the West, significant numbers of troops only began to assemble once the King had established himself at Shrewsbury. By the eve of Edgehill, the King had been able to add to his existing infantry the regiments of Charles Gerard's, Sir Lewis Dyve's, Thomas Blagge's, Richard Fielding's, Sir Thomas Lunsford's, Richard Rolle's, Sir Edward Fitton's, Sir Edward Stradling's, Sir John Beaumont's, Sir Gilbert Gerard's, Lord Molyneaux's, the Earl of Northampton's, Earl River's and Sir Thomas Salisbury's, the latter infamously described by Robert Evans as 'twelve hundred poor Welsh vermin'.

Unlike Essex's army prior to Edgehill, there was no evidence that Royalist regiments received items of uniform clothing, or any items of clothing at all. Rather, the only source of identification for the Royalists in the early months was the tradition of using ribbons, in this case red or scarlet, worn either

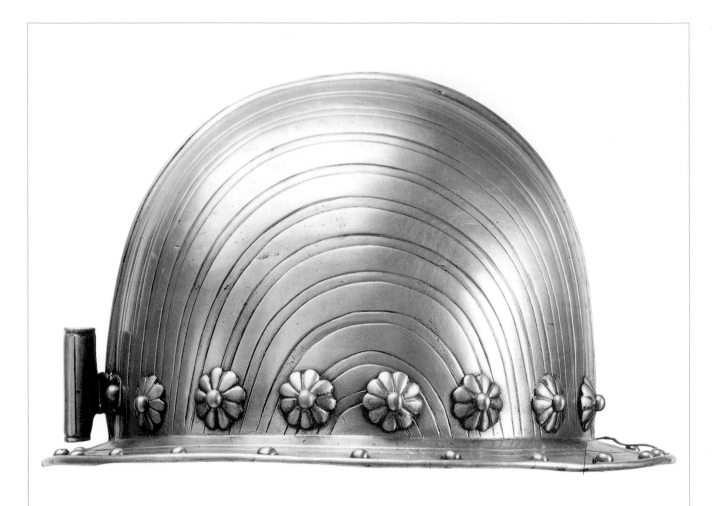

Side view of a fluted Flemish or French infantry morion c.1610 of the style worn by pikemen. The Trustees of the Wallace Collection, A68.

on their civilian coats or on their headgear. Evidence for this came in a report from the Venetian ambassador to the Doge just after Edgehill where he stated that the Royalists could be identified by 'rose-coloured bands on their hats'.

The fundamental inhibiting factor for the King for any earlier concentration was providing armaments and equipment, a matter stressed by the King's faithful minister and later historian, Edward Hyde, the Earl of Clarendon. Allowances must be made for the fact Clarendon wrote his gloomy observations as to the standard of Royalist armament and equipment long after the war when it served to stress the actual disparity. Nonetheless, he undoubtedly reflected the desperate reality of the situation when he pointed out that 'The king was exceedingly disappointed in his expectation of arms from Holland', only '800 muskets, 500 pairs of pistols and 200 swords' was landed by *The Providence*, the initial proceeds of the Queen's attempt at pawning the Crown Jewels (in practice it proved very difficult to find Dutch merchants who had sufficient funds to pawn the jewels with). With little else, including powder, in his magazine 'he was

compelled to begin at Nottingham, and so in all places as he passed, to borrow the arms from the train-bands'. Inevitably, not all were happy at their county magazines being denuded in this manner and certainly in Yorkshire and Shropshire 'there was none of that kind of borrowing. Although the King had hoped to receive considerable quantities of weapons from 'the noblemen and gentlemen of quality....such supplies of arms out of their own armouries' were described by Clarendon as being 'very mean'. Nonetheless, by the eve of Edgehill, 'by all these means together, the foot, (all but three or four hundred who marched without any weapons but a cudgel,) were armed with musket, and bags for their powder, and pikes; but in the whole there was not one pikeman had a corslet, and very few musketeers who had swords'.

In the weeks after Edgehill the actual number of musket available was specifically detailed, the Ordnance papers specifying that for the march on London in November, powder for 4,000 musket was issued. Given that the army numbered around 12,000, having deducted the horse, it would appear that the ratio of musket to pike was at best 1:1, thus suggesting that at Edgehill the ratio was, if anything, probably less.

As with Parliament's army, it initially fell to the

Zischagge helmet in the East European style, but actually probably French c.1630-1640. Very fashionable amongst veterans of the Continental wars. The Trustees of the Wallace Collection, A102.

captains of each troop of horse to do their best to obtain sufficient equipment and as with Essex's troopers, the reality fell short of the ideal. As before, Clarendon's observations were generally negative. He commented of the initial 800 horse the King assembled that 'few better armed than with swords'. By the eve of Edgehill he did not find matters had improved as 'Amongst the horse, the officers had their full desire if they were able to procure old backs and breasts and pots, with pistols or carbines for their two or three first ranks, and swords for the rest; themselves (and some soldiers by their examples) having gotten besides their pistols and swords, a short poleaxe'. Not all troopers though were so poorly equipped given some officers had access to well stocked private arsenals. Back in July, an observer at Beverley noted a troop who had ridden to join the King on 'fifty great horses all of a darke Bay, handsomely set out with ash-colour'd ribbins, every man gentilely accoutred, and

98 The Royal Army 1642-46

Opposite and above.

These recreated blue coated musketeers of Hopton's Regiment of the King's Army could as easily be any blue coated regiment who received suits from the Oxford distribution in July 1643. English Heritage.

armed. They were presented to His Majesty, but it was not knowne from whom certainly, but supposed from the Earl of Newcastle, by the bravery of their accoutrements'.

As with Parliament's horse, there were very few references to clothing for the Royalist cavalry troopers, although as with the former, grey and red apparently predominated. This was implied in a London merchants record just prior to the storming of the bridge at Brentford in November 1642 when 'Prince Rupert took off his scarlet coat, which was very rich, and gave it to his man, and buckled on his arms and put a grey coate over it, that he might not be discovered'. One assumes Rupert would only thus have been inconspicuous if his men wore clothes of a similar hue. Whatever their standards of equipment and clothes, Rupert did a better job of organising and training the disparate troops into coherent regiments when compared to Essex's, as proved in combat at Powick Bridge and Edgehill.

The Royalist War Effort

The lull in fighting from December onwards was the conventional period when armies retired to their winter quarters to re-equip and recruit. Given Parliament's early advantage in equipment thanks to Hull, the first half of 1643 ironically witnessed an apparently more organised, determined and effective effort by the Royalists to provide their growing forces with sufficient arms and equipment. Despite the fact that most of England's established armaments industry was firmly under Parliamentary control in the iron producing region of the Weald and the gunshops of the Minories, by 1642 the iron industry was not confined to the South-East with the Forest of Dean, South Wales and the West Midlands as major rivals. These iron-producing areas were securely in royalist hands, and the production of domestic ironware and nails was soon replaced by the manufacture of pike-heads, swords and muskets for the King.

Equally, on the face of it, the manufacture of gunpowder would seem to have been in Parliament's favour. Up to 1640 the making of gunpowder had been a royal monopoly, free import or unlicensed home manufacture was forbidden. Authorised production was largely confined to the same region of

100 The Royal Army 1642-46

These demi-culverins would have normally seen service at the many sieges of the Civil Wars. English Heritage.

South-East England as the original gun-foundries and again within easy reach of the Tower. In fact, much of this royal monopoly was under the control of one family, the Evelyns. But the Bishops' Wars which had vastly increased demands for powder and the subsequent growth of political opposition had undermined royal control with many illicit powder makers setting-up. It must be remembered that, unlike the iron industry with its requirement for substantial plant, gunpowder could be milled cheaply in a small way by hand. In August 1641, the Long Parliament forced an end to the royal monopoly so that 'every man that will might make gunpowder', and that it could be imported freely. Ironically, this worked in Charles' favour as it undermined the viability of the Evelyn family's authorised production, causing them to substantially reduce their output, while the many small and illicit powdermakers were to become a vital source of powder for Charles as they flocked to

Opposite.
This recreated yellow coated musketeer, possibly from an Irish regiment, has just lit his match. English Heritage.

Oxford to take advantage of the commercial opportunity.

Generally, in respect of the supply of gunpowder, although some commentators have suggested the King faced critical shortages at key points during the war, there is no evidence this was due to an overall lack of availability. There was no doubt that at the commencement of the conflict there were problems which influenced strategic decisions. In November 1642 there was just seventeen tons of blackpowder in store. The army's 4,000 musketeers required 2,000lb, that was 1/2lb for each musketeer for 'his bandiliers full'. Although this left sixteen tons, this was insufficient to both supply the 27 field pieces whilst maintaining an adequate reserve to re-supply the musketeers once their initial twelve to fifteen individual charges were expended. This apparently played a crucial role in persuading Charles to retire rather than chance his arm by attacking Essex's men and the London Trained Bands drawn up on Turnham Green. By 1643, Royalist supplies had improved and although at the First Battle of Newbury, the King's 17 to 18 guns were silent for much of the battle. This though was due to a failure of powder and shot to arrive in time from Oxford 26 miles away, rather than there being a strategic shortage. Equally, in the

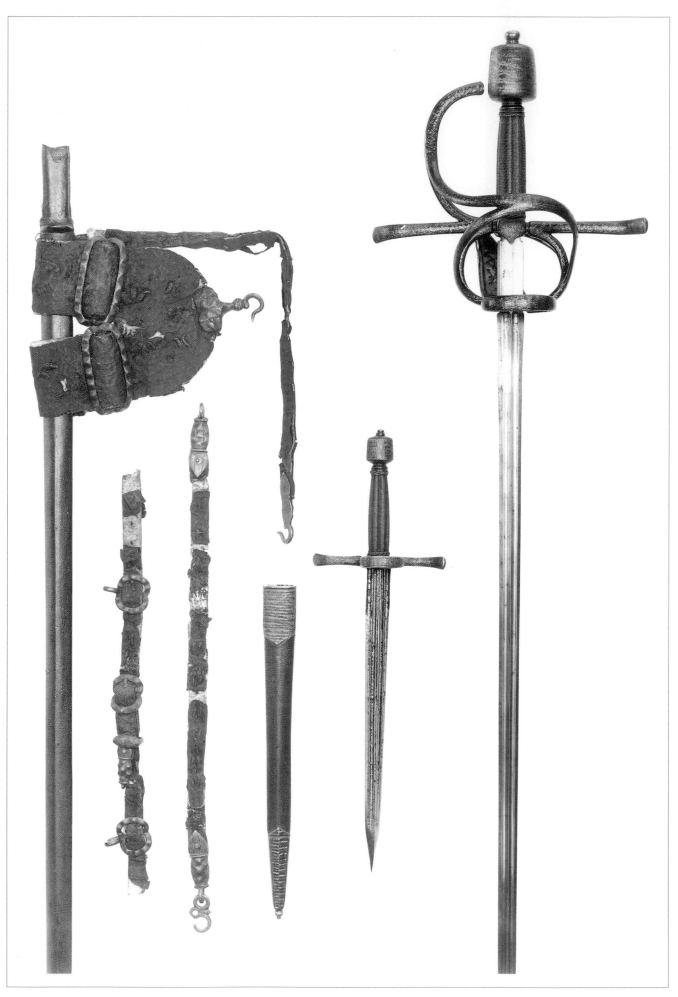

Officer's hanger and belt only (the belt has separated into two parts), German c.1620. The Trustees of the Wallace Collection, A575.

summer of 1644 both the King near Oxford and Rupert operating out of Shrewsbury complained of a lack of gunpowder and in October 1644 the King complained of shortages of small arms with the army. Yet in all instances the Ordinance records clearly demonstrate there were ample quantities of powder, shot and arms in store. As so often in the history of warfare, distribution proved to be the weak link.

With it becoming clear in December 1642 that it was going to be a long war, Charles set about establishing the means to wage one. Although six of the nine senior officers of the pre-war Ordinance Office had remained loyal to the King and joined him in Oxford, a completely new Ordnance organisation had to be constructed as all the secretaries had remained in London. To assist the new Ordnance Office based in Oxford, Charles turned to various

Opposite.
Officer's swept hilt rapier, sheath, belt, hanger, dagger and sheath, all German c.1620. The Trustees of the Wallace Collection, A575.

prominent refugees from the City of London's merchant class who had thrown in their lot with the King. Over the next twelve months, the new Ordnance Office was able to create a substantial arms industry, making the best possible use of Oxford's resources. A foundry was set up at Christ Church College with the Ordnance Commissioners having authority to seize supplies of metal wherever they could be found. A mill for boring ordnance was fitted out, by order of the Council of War in the summer of 1643, with tools to grind sword-blades. The complementary process of forging the blades was undertaken at Gloucester Hall. For powder, new mills were built and old mills adapted along the banks of the rivers Isis and Cherwell. This crucial industry was organised in its early stages by William Baber, a Bristol powdermaker who, ironically had been proscribed by the King back in 1637 for producing powder without a royal licence. With the aid of his son and uncle, who had also been outlawed in the 1630s for illicit powdermaking, and another Bristol man, Baber set up his works and started production by January 1643. But Oxford's output ultimately fell short of the 50 barrels per week envisaged due to shortage of both money and raw materials.

Oxford though was not the only centre for royalist

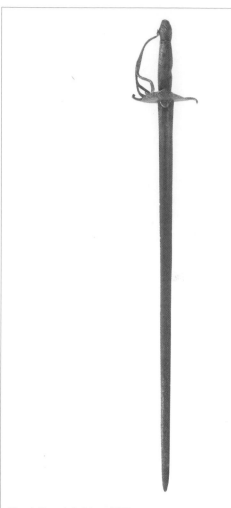

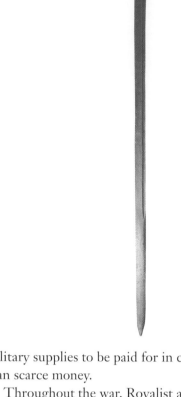

Top left and right.

A simple proto-mortuary pattern sword made by Jencks of Hounslow. Gunnersbury Park Museum.

production. The Midlands and Gloucestershire not only produced considerable quantities of iron and muskets, but also match and gunpowder, with Worcester being the main point of manufacturing. Most fundamental though to maintaining Royalist armies was the taking of Bristol in July 1643 which rapidly became a centre for manufacture, foreign importation and a point of entry into the Royalist supply lines for the military products of a wide area. By May 1645, the Bristol manufacturer Richard March was able to offer 15,000 muskets and 5,000 pikes per year although a lack of funds meant this abundant source could not be fully utilised. Hopton's conquest of the West also made available the manufacturing centres of Bath, Wells and Devizes. By the winter of 1643, Wells alone was producing 15 barrels of powder per week, although again, supply was restricted by financial limitations. Lacking readily available funds to always take advantage of domestic manufacture, the Royalist hold on Newcastle and later Bristol provided an added advantage in that these ports' peacetime commodities enabled imported

military supplies to be paid for in corn and coal rather than scarce money.

Throughout the war, Royalist armies relied on imported powder, weapons and equipment from France, the Low Countries and to a lesser extent Ireland, to make up the shortfalls from domestic manufacture. At the commencement of hostilities, the King's supporters held only two major ports, Chester and Newcastle, with only the latter being situated to receive supplies from the Continent. In addition, Parliament's control of the navy enabled some cargoes to be intercepted. In 1643 a shipment from Denmark of 2,977 muskets, 3,000 musket rests, 493 pair of pistols, 1,500 pikes, 3,040 swords, 3,000 helmets, 476 barrels of gunpowder, 990 bundles of match and a small cask of pistol keys was seized. But thanks to a series of battlefield victories and storms, by mid-1643, Bristol and the West Coast in general were in Royalist hands and, by Christmas 1643, the strategically placed Weymouth was available to receive supplies. In fact,

Opposite.

English musket-proof 'munition' breastplate for a harquebusier, from a manor house in Sussex, together with a harquebusier's 'three bar pot' lobster-tailed helmet. David Edge, Histrionix Living History Group.

106 The Royal Army 1642-46

even before Christmas 1642, the Dutch merchant, John Van Haesdonck, who became one of the King's major gunrunners during the course of the war, had contracted to deliver to Tynemouth, 3,000 muskets, 2,000 pairs of pistols, 3,000 sword blades, 1,000 carbines with fire-locks, 20 tons of match and 1,000 hand grenades. As if to symbolise this improving situation, in February, a year after her departure, the Queen landed at Bridlington Bay in Yorkshire with the bulk of the supplies she had been assembling in Holland. This included some 10,000 arms, 32 cannon, a vital 78 barrels of blackpowder and sundry other items. Having distributed parts of this cargo to Newcastle's troops, the importance of this shipment was indicated by the successful efforts made to escort the convey into Oxford on 14 July. Apart from five regiments of foot which accompanied it and the Queen south from Yorkshire, the King himself with

troops from the Oxford garrison rode out to meet it at Edgehill.

After the Cessation in Ireland in September 1643, alongside the transfer of English troops, considerable quantities of military supplies poured into Chester, Bristol and Weymoth from the arsenals stocked by Parliament to reconquer the Irish. Yet the quantities of material received from the Irish arsenals was negligible compared to the materials brought in from the Continent. In this crucial matter several wealthy City of London merchants who had joined the King as refugees, such as Sir Nicholas Crispe, played a vital role as gun-runners. An example of the quantities being brought in came in a report of February 1644 from Weymouth by Captain John Strachen of the Ordnance Office where he listed the safe arrival of 4917 muskets, 4202 bandoleers, 322 pikes, 314 barrels of powder and raw materials for powder making, tow and brimstone. But an important caveat to this was that he stressed that the quantity of stores delivered was far more impressive than the quality and he refused to pay high prices for inferior material he described as 'old common powder that hath lyen in some magazine these 4, or 5 years....musketts....of 3, or 4 score sundry bores....and all the old trash that could bee rapt together'. An even larger Flemish cargo

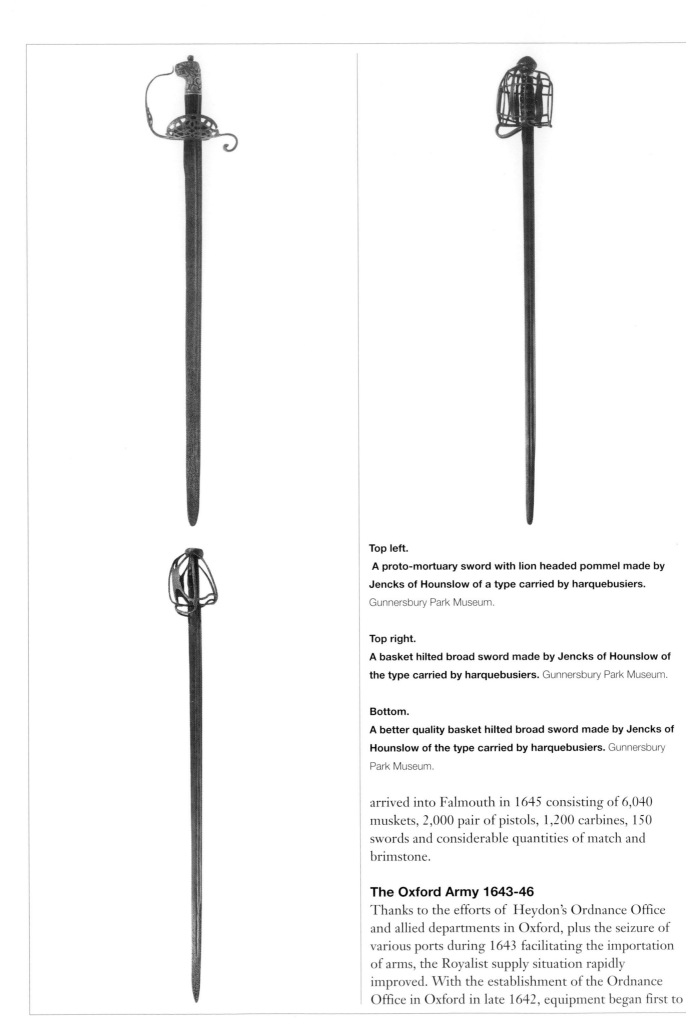

Top left.

A proto-mortuary sword with lion headed pommel made by Jencks of Hounslow of a type carried by harquebusiers. Gunnersbury Park Museum.

Top right.

A basket hilted broad sword made by Jencks of Hounslow of the type carried by harquebusiers. Gunnersbury Park Museum.

Bottom.

A better quality basket hilted broad sword made by Jencks of Hounslow of the type carried by harquebusiers. Gunnersbury Park Museum.

arrived into Falmouth in 1645 consisting of 6,040 muskets, 2,000 pair of pistols, 1,200 carbines, 150 swords and considerable quantities of match and brimstone.

The Oxford Army 1643-46

Thanks to the efforts of Heydon's Ordnance Office and allied departments in Oxford, plus the seizure of various ports during 1643 facilitating the importation of arms, the Royalist supply situation rapidly improved. With the establishment of the Ordnance Office in Oxford in late 1642, equipment began first to

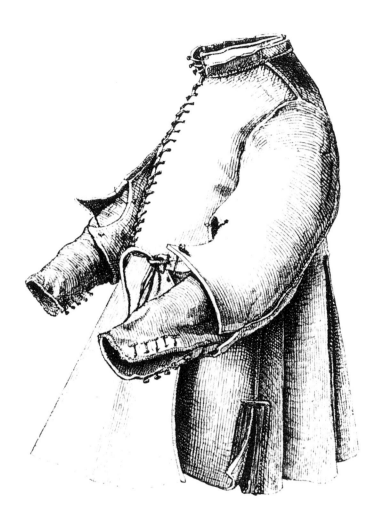

This drawing of Colonel Brooke's buff coat represents a typical officer's version of this item. The actual coat was sadly destroyed by fire in Warwick Castle in 1871. PEW.

be issued for the horse, although a proportion of troopers were still going short and as with Parliament, buff-coats do not appear to have been issued in any significant numbers. On 14th December 1642, Captain Gerard Croker's troop of 44 men received:

> Backs......33
> Brests.......33
> Potts.........33
> Vambraces one pre. Gauntletts. 2.
> Holdsters..13 pre.
> Gorgetts....25.

By 16th February 1643, Heydon was already able to order to be delivered to Captain Bernard De Gommes company of Colonel Blagge's Regiment of Foot 'forty Musquetts, Bandaliers, and thirty Pikes'. By April/May 1643, the regiments at the Abingdon Camp were receiving considerably more equipment, with the ratio of musket to pike reaching the required 2:1.

In this Victorian rendering of the Battle of Brentford, Prince Rupert leads his troopers against the barricade defended by a troop of dismounted Parliamentary horse. Hounslow Local Studies Department.

Over the next year or so production of all categories of equipment soared. The early expedient of utilising powder bags rather than bandoleers, despite the former being far less watertight, continued well into1644. This was possibly because Oxford offered a ready supply of appropriately skilled craftsmen, it being ordered on 30th June that from His Majesties stores there be issued 'to Richard Harte bookebinder...Calfe skinns tanned & oyled for Powder baggs'. On 14th June it was ordered that it be delivered to 'Sariant Maiour Bischip Sariant Maiour of the Tertia Comaunded by the Lord Vicownt Grandeson a hundred leather bags for the Musqueters of yt Tertia'. On 7th July, Heydon ordered to be dispatched to the King's armies 'Leaguer at Abington', '200 Powder Baggs for Musketers wth Girdles & Hangers for Swords and fforty Bandoleres'. The mix of powder bags and bandoleers was much the same for dragoons. On 16th June Colonel Washington's Dragoons received 36 'Baggs wth Girdles & Hangers to yem'. Having said this, certain senior officers'

regiments appear to have been somewhat better catered for as on 14th July it was ordered that 'fforty Musketts yt: are ffixt and ffit for seruice with bandeleers...ffor the supplyinge of Prince Ruperts Regimt: of Dragooners comanded by Coll: Enis'. Yet with the infantry, as late as 9th May 1644, the company of Captain-Lieutenant John Forster of the King's Lifeguard of Foot received an issue of 27 powder bags and 13 bandoleers. By late 1644 no further issues of powder bags were made, only bandoleers being issued.

Whilst the infantry received adequate arms and equipment, and despite an order on 14th December 1642 by the Council of War that 'Musketts for dragoons'...'to be but 3 foot longe' were to be manufactured, most dragoons had to make do with standard infantry matchlocks for much of the war although by late 1644 some of the more favoured regiments began to receive at least a proportion of firelocks. On 5th November it was directed that 'Sr: Thomas Hooper Knight...receive...Thirty Musquetts

Opposite.
Lacking sufficient bandoleers, a very significant proportion of musketeers on both sides, but particularly for the King, began the war with powder bags for their cartridges. Partizan Press.

These demi-culverins would have normally seen service at the many sieges of the Civil Wars. English Heritage.

with snaphances towards the Armeing of the Regiment of Dragooners of Our Deare Nephewe Prince Rupert'.

In terms of clothing for the infantry, matters witnessed a dramatic improvement. That the King's forces began to receive substantial quantities of uniform sets of cloths in mid-1643 there was no doubt. In January 1643, tailors in and around Oxford were ordered to produce 5,000 coats. Further, on 6th March 1643 Thomas Bushell, an established Royalist entrepreneur and activist undertook, 'he would procure for the King's Souldiers Cassocks, Breeches, Stockings & Capps at reasonable rates to be delivered at Oxford'. This order went on to detail the mechanism by which these items would be provided as 'at the delivery to receyve readye money, or a bill of exchange to be payd at London, the choyce to be left to them who provide the clothes. And when one Loade of Clothes is brought, or in bringing, to go on with providing of a second Loade, and so from time to time till the Kings Army be all provided for, and payd for in such manner as before'.

By 12th June, Bushell had already made substantial deliveries to the King's Lifeguard (as well as having assisted in raising them in the first place) and three other regiments, and this and his many other services were attested to on behalf of the King, 'the many true services you have actually done us in these times of trying a subjects loyalty: as in raiseing us the Derbyshire Minors for our Life Guard at our first entrance to this warr for our owne defence; when the Lord Lieutenant of that Countie refused to appear in the service: supplyinge us at Shrewsbury and Oxford with your Mint for the payment of our Armye, when all the Officers in the Mint of our Tower of London forsook their attendance....your changing the dollars with wch wee paid our Souldiers at six shillings a piece, when the malignant partee cried them down at ffive your stopping the Mutinie in Shropshire when the soldiers had left their arrears uppon the Countrye, and brought the associacion of the Gentrie to perfeccion; your providing us one hundred tonnes of lead shot for our Army without money, when we paid

Opposite.
After the distribution in Oxford in July 1643 of uniform suits of clothes consisting of monteros, coats and breeches, many of the King's army would have resembled this musketeer. Partizan Press.

Although showing signs of wear and tear this late war royalist musketeer remains well equipped. Partizan Press.

before twentie pounds per tonne; and your helpinge us to twenty six pieces of ordinance when wee were at a straight for supplying of Chester, Shrewsbury and other places; your cloathing our liefe Guard and three regiments more, with suites, stockings, shoes, and mounteroes when wee were readie to march in the ffield: your invention for our better knowinge and rewarding the Forlorne Hope with Badges of Silver at your own charge when the soldiers were ready to run away through the instigation of some disafected persons: your contractinge with Merchants beyond the Seas, for providing good quantities of powder, pistoll, carbine, muskett and bullet, in exchange for your owne commodities, when wee were wantinge of such ammunicion: with divers other severall services which we hope our royall successors will never forget'.

Between the tailors of Oxford and Mr.Bushell, by 15th July the Oxford antiquarian Anthony Wood recorded that, 'all the common soldiers then at Oxford were newe apparrelled, some all in red, coates, breeches and mounteers; & some all in blewe'. The regiments that Wood refers to were the fourteen 'all very weake' that formed the King's Oxford army and

which departed Oxford on 18th July under Rupert to lay siege to Bristol, namely the Lord General's, Lord Molyneaux's, Gilbert Gerrard's, Ralph Dutton's, John Owen's, Jacob Astley's, Edward Fitton's, Richard Bolles', Richrd Herbert's, John Belasyse's, Edward Stradling's, Henry Lunsford's and Charles Lloyd's. While precisely which of these regiment received red and which blue suits was not recorded, there was evidence from other sources for certain of them. Both Lunsford's (later Prince Rupert's), and Sir Michael Woodhouse's (later the Prince of Wales' Lifeguard of Foot), who briefly joined the Oxford army at this time, were recorded in the Shrewsbury billeting records for 1643 as being 'Blewcotes'. As Lunsford's were undoubtedly recorded as wearing blue coats in 1644 and 1645, it seems a fair surmise this regimental coat colour dated from July 1643. In Oxford, the King's Lifeguard were recorded by Sir Samuel Luke on 14th November as, 'There are 100 redd coates of the Kings life guard left in Oxford'. Astley's was also recorded as wearing red coats. Equally, again apparently benefiting from this distribution as part of the Oxford garrison were Charles Gerrard's who were recorded as blue coats. Five other regiments who were apparently clothed from this distribution were those forming the escort of the Queen's convoy of arms which arrived in Oxford on 15th July, namely The Queen's Lifeguard of Foot, Thomas Blackwell's, Thomas Tyldsley's, William Eure's and Conyers D'Arcy's. Of these, The Queen's Lifeguard was recorded as being in red, possibly to match the King's Lifeguard, while D'Arcy's were referred to as 'Blue Coats'. Finally, although formed just after the storming of Bristol, Lord Hopton's regiment were referred to as blue coats, probably being in receipt of surplus cloths from the Oxford distribution a few weeks before.

In fact red, blue and white/grey appear to have been the predominant colours of the suits and coats generally issued to the King's forces. On 13th November 1643, Luke recorded as marching through Buckingham, '200 Blew coates, 200 grey coats and 200 red coates', some on their way to Oxford and others to join Sir Ralph Hopton. Equally, Symonds noted in Oxford on 13th February 1644, both the King and Queen's Lifeguards as being clothed in red, Sir Charles Gerrard's in blue and Pinchbeck's (later Bard's) in grey. The last of these regiments had originally marched south from Newcastle's forces in the north acting as guards to a convoy of arms earlier in the year. Grey, or undyed natural wool appears to have been the predominate colour of Newcastle's northern foot, reflecting the local availability or lack of dyes. During the siege of York, 'some of the

The trail of this demi-culverin would have been harnessed to a team of horses to move it into position or on the march. English Heritage.

Marquesse of Newcastle, his souldiers were taken prisoner also; they had white coats...'. At Marston Moor,'There was one entire regiment of foot belonging to Newcastle, called the lambs, because they were all new clothed in white woolen cloth'.

Red, blue and grey/white though were not the only coat colours worn by Royalist infantry. Regiments arriving from Ireland appear to have worn a mixture of yellow and green, again reflecting the easy availability of these particular dye colours in Ireland and the north-east of England where many were landed and re-clothed. A member of the Parliamentarian garrison of Wardour Castle, Edmund Ludlow, recorded during the Royalist assault in January 1644 that, 'those who stormed my side were the Irish yellow-coats, commanded by Captain Leicester'. The captain was an officer in Colonel Matthew Appleyard's, an English regiment recently returned from Ireland. Also referred to as yellow coats was the Irish regiment of Colonel John Talbot, raised in late 1643. Another regiment arriving from Ireland was Colonel Henry Tillier's which landed at Neston in Cheshire on 7th February

1644. It was a composite formation, drawn as Symonds recorded from, 'Colonel Sir Charles Coote...Col Sir Henry Tichbourne...Lord Lambert, Lord Burlacy, Irish regiments, These four regiments were raysed about and in Dublyn...Some of these came over with Tilyard, 1,000 foot greencoates came with him, most of them lost at Yorke with Prince Rupert'. In fact, at Marston Moor both Newcastle's whitecoats and Tillier's greencoats were sufficiently distinguished to be commented upon by the victors, who, generally wearing red, the popular paper 'A True Relation of the Victory' reported that, 'A Regiment of Redcoats...' and 'Major-General Lesley charged the Earl of Newcastles brigade of Whitecoats...and after them charged a brigade of Green-coats'. Confirming that Tillier's wore green and that Rupert's Regiment wore blue was a reference to both in a letter of Thomas Dallison to Rupert of 4th August. At the time, both regiments were being effectively re-raised in the Welsh Marches after the debacle at Marston Moor, to which Dallison commented, 'I have had 113 coats and caps for foot

Following pages.
Assorted wheel-lock pistols, all first half of the 17th century, typical of those carried by the cavalry. The Trustees of the Wallace Collection, A1157, '60, '62 and '80.

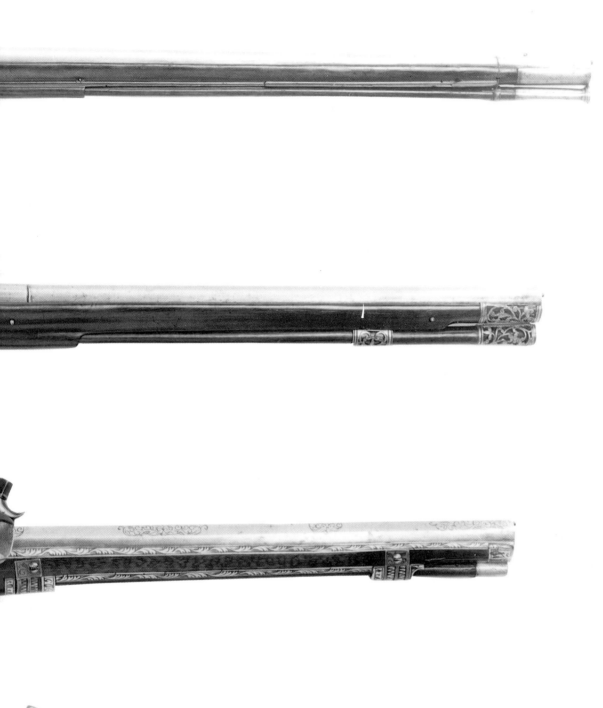

This recreated musketeer is charging his piece from a bandoleer. English Heritage.

soldiers in the house of my Lord Powis, an 100 of which are blue, which will serve very well for your Highness's regiment of foot. The rest are green, which may serve for Col. Tylyer's'.

Whilst the issuing of uniform sets of clothing ought to have negated the need to wear ribbons for identification, as late as 30th August 1643, John Malet found it necessary to write to his friend, Captain George Trevelyan, 'I understand...of a desire you had to put your colours upon your coats for the better knowing of your men, which if you do, in mine opinion would much wrong the coat. The differences that Captains use in the wars is in the arming of his pikes for the pikemen, which is to be of his colours, and likewise the fringe of the headpiece of the shot for the shot. The daubing of a coat with lace of sundry colours, as some do use them, I do neither take to be soldierlike nor profitable for the coat. If a Captain miscarry, he that cometh in his room, his colours being contrary, tears off the former and puts in his own, and by this means often times tears coat and all. Myself have resolved for my company in such sort as I have written unto you, which I desire might be all

your good likings.'

Despite these sentiments, at least a few regiments continued to attach ribbons, particularly in the North. When a number of the Marquis of Newcastle's men were captured during the siege of York in June 1644, some had white coats 'with crosses on the sleeves, wrought with red and blew silk, an ensign wee conceive of some Po(p)ish regiment'. There is equally an intriguing portrait by Dobson of Prince Rupert with Colonels William Murray and John Russell, where Russell is depicted dipping a pink, black and silver grey ribbon into a glass of wine. This apparently represents the moment when Russell ceremonially received his commission as lieutenant-colonel of Rupert's regiment and the ribbon was in fact the regimental ribbon of the Prince's Regiment, particularly as the regimental colours, designed by the Prince himself, was a unique combination of silver grey, black and white.

Having been issued uniform suits of clothing in a single colour, these clothes were inevitably reduced to rags within a few months by the rigours of campaigning. Whilst some regiments, such as Rupert's, Tillier's and the King's Lifeguard undoutedly received replacement clothes in the same colour, others had to accept what was on offer, essentially relying on the suits provided at any given issue. A clear example of a regiment effectively changing the colour of their coats were Sir Ralph Dutton's. Being part of the Oxford army in July 1643 they were undoubtedly in either red or blue suits for that distribution. Having subsequently become Sir Stephen Hawkins' regiment they had received in 1644 replacements of a different colour as during the relief of Basing House in September 1644, Colonel Henry Gage recorded that he briefly left 'in the House 100 White-Coats of Collonel Hawkins' Regiment'. Equally, in September 1644, having destroyed the Earl of Essex's army at Lostwithiel, the King's Oxford army received new clothing while marching back through Devon. Having ordered the County of Devon to provide 3,000 suits, along with equal pairs of shoes and stockings 'against the Winter' on the 18th, Edward Walker recorded that these were received within a week and a half between the 23rd and 30th at Chard in Somerset. Given the rapidity by which this quantity of clothing was assembled much of it must have been civilian clothing with the balance manufactured from whatever

Opposite.
Writing an order at his field desk, this recreated officer is fashionably dressed in the most elegant of styles reflecting his location in a garrison. English Heritage.

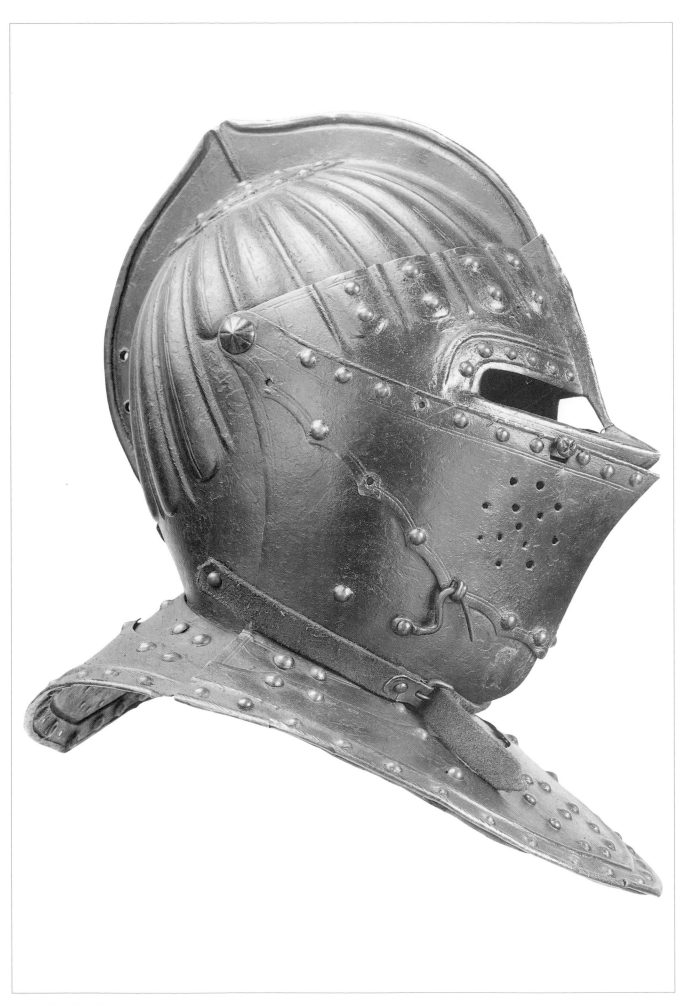

mix of cloth was available. This might help explain the continued practice of wearing ribbons for identification.

Mention should be made here of the common confusion some writers have had between contemporary references to coat colours and to 'colours', meaning regimental flags. For example, whilst Rupert's regiment of foot undoubtedly wore blue it is equally certain they flew Rupert's unique black flags as clearly referred to by Symonds at the storming of Leicester, 'Colonel John Russell, with the Prince's regiment of blew cotes, and also the Prince's fferelockes, assaulted. They set the Prince's black colours on the great battery within'. Three further quotes make abundantly clear that the contemporary term 'colour' meant flag. From a newspaper report of 28th October 1643, in the Thomason Tracts regarding a skirmish between Royalist troops of the Oxford garrison and Parliamentarians from Northampton, '...to whom was joined 700 foote, choice men, ten or more out of every company in and about Oxford, they were 300 Red coates, and 200 blue coates, and 200 mixed coloured coates, but no colours or ensignes amongst hem being a commanded party'. Equally, Luke on 25 December 1643, recorded one of his informants seeing '...12 or 13 collours of horse and 6 collours of foote under the command of the Earle Rivers...'. Back in July, having arrived in Oxford to be issued red or blue suits, Thomas Blackwell's regiment was referred to as 'The Queen's black regiment under Colonel Blackwell'. Unfortunately, many later writers have wrongly interpreted both latter quotes as meaning Earl Rivers and Blackwell's both wore black coats, a highly unlikely situation given black was the most expensive dye colour available as compared to the cheapness of red, blue or simply undyed wool.

From the handful of surviving references for the clothing of the Royalist Horse, red was also apparently their predominant colour. On 4th August 1644, the commander of Prince Rupert's Regiment of Horse, Colonel Sir Thomas Dallison, wrote to him confirming he had 'three or four hundred yards of cloth, which may serve to make coats or cloaks for your Highness' regiment of horse'.

As with Parliament, by early 1644 there were no noticeable shortages in clothes, equipment or arms, for the King and the army which fought at Naseby a year later was in all respects well equipped. As with Parliament's armies, the proportion of musketeers to pikeman rose significantly, there being by 1644 a number of all-musket regiments, Lord Inchiquin's red coated Irish regiment, Sir Henry Bard's Foot and possibly including Rupert's own regiment of foot. In February 1644 the Ordnance Office in Oxford noted, 'Concerning the 1100 Musketts to bee reserved for Prince Rupert. There hath bine deliuered by a former warrt from hence to his Regiment 700 Musketts, and Bandeleeres, and haue nowe received a warrt from my Lord for 500 newe Musketts wth Bandeleeres'. As with Parliament, Royalist musketeers discarded the antiquated musket rests early on, few if any being issued after the summer of 1643. Equally, the use of armour for the infantry effectively ended, with few Royalist pikemen receiving even helmets after 1643, and whilst armour remained the main defence for the horse, buff-coated troopers were far from the norm.

As the tide of war turned against the King in the summer and autumn of 1645, most of the key ports were either cut off by siege or fell to the all conquering New Model Army. Newcastle was cut off by the Scots as early as January 1644 and by late 1645 Weymouth and Bristol were back in Parliamentary hands whilst Chester and the West Country were effectively cut off from Oxford. Yet the equally dramatic diminution in the size of the Royalist forces meant that the remaining domestic sources were sufficient to ensure clothes, equipment and arms until the end of the war. The King did not lose the war because he ran short of material, he ran short of manpower long before. By 1646, the arsenals of Oxford held more weapons and powder than there were soldiers' hands to put them in.

New Styles of Warfare 1646-1660

In terms of military evolution, most writers tend to consider the fourteen years following the surrender of Charles I to the Scots at Newark in May 1646 as little more than a series of ever more desperate attempts by the English Royalists, the Scots and Irish to challenge the all conquering army of Oliver Cromwell. Apart from narrative accounts of the campaigns and battles, little or no attention is paid to the continuing development of England's powerful military machine. Yet during these years the army grew to a strength of some 72,000 men, a figure not to be surpassed until the last decade of the century. Further, alongside the familiar fields of England and the Lowlands of Scotland, elements of this standing army had to adapt to disparate methods of warfare and theatres as far apart as the guerrilla campaigns in the Highlands of Scotland and the wet lands of Ireland, the mosquito infested Caribbean and the flat fields of Flanders. Inevitably, alongside adaptations in combat methods, this had an impact on weapons, equipment and clothes.

Firelocks

By the conclusion of the First Civil War the army was coated in red and equipped to the familiar ratio of 2:1 in terms of musket to pike. In the subsequent campaigns of the Second and Third Civil Wars, be it at Preston in 1648, Dunbar in 1650 or finally Worcester in 1651, there was little change. This could not be said for the subsequent fighting which dragged on long after the last set-piece battles were over. In both Ireland and the Highlands of Scotland resistance continued well into the mid-1650s involving the English army in bitter guerrilla warfare. This resulted in the building of fortifications, equivalent to modern firebases, and a war of ambuscade and counter insurgency sweeps by small units. The most obvious change this brought about was the rapid increase in the proportion of firelocks, in all respects the technological weapon of the future.

By the end of the Civil War the use of firelocks in the New Model Army was not specifically limited to specialist companies as the proportion of firelocks in every regiment of foot increased. The Ordnance Papers record for the equipping of the New Model Army between 1645-46, over 3,300 firelock muskets being delivered, far in excess of the number needed by the 200 Artillery Train Guards of Major Desborough or the 1,200 men of Colonel Okey's Dragoons, even accounting for replacements due to losses in the field. Further, there was a clear distinction between shorter and cheaper dragoon muskets and standard firelocks for the infantry. In the Ordnance Papers the former were specifically referred to as 'snaphaunce Dragoones full bore' at '12s 4d' each, of which only 224 were ordered, many of Okey's men still being in possession of their original firelocks. The latter were specified as 'Snaphance Musketts full bore & proofe & foure foote longe' at '15s 6d' each, being the description of the balance of over 3,000 firelocks. That a number of firelock muskets were issued to every regiment of foot was illustrated by a regimental return of May 1650 when Colonel Walton's company was re-equipped and issued with 66 matchlocks and 6 firelocks. These were almost certainly for sentry duty to both save on match and avoid tell-tale light. Assuming a similar proportion to each of a regiment's ten companies (10 to the larger Colonel's and Lieutenant-Colonel's companies and 8 to the Major's company) a regiment would have had around 80 to 100 firelocks. With twelve regiments of foot in the original New Model Army, the 3,000 plus firelocks would have been more than sufficient. In fact, this practice was apparently already evolving prior to 1645, as on 15th November 1643, an official return for the arms necessary to equip Colonel Edward Harley's regiment of Foot to its regulation strength of 1,200 men recorded a requirement of 800 muskets of which 150 were to be firelocks.

Equally, with the Scots army after 1646, firelocks became more widely distributed. At Preston in 1648,

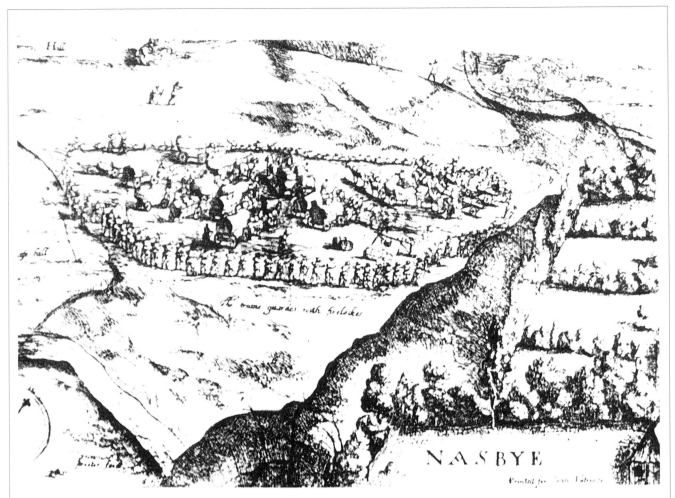

At the bottom left hand corner of Sprigg's illustration of Naseby in *Anglia Rediviva,* the firelocks are shown encircling the baggage and train. PEW.

Sir Alexander Fraser of Philorth's Aberdeenshire regiment were fully equipped with firelocks. At Dunbar in 1650, Cromwell's dawn assault caught most of the Scottish infantry with their match un-lit and only two Scottish regiments were able to return fire, Cambell of Lawers and Sir John Haldane of Gleneggies, both of whom were fully equipped with firelocks.

The Ordnance Papers after 1646 demonstrate a continuing high level of firelocks being ordered and delivered to the army. Some would appear to have been for specific firelock companies. For example, in 1647 it was listed that two un-regimented companies of firelocks were landed in Dublin. Yet the return for Colonel Walton's company indicated that a proportion were being issued to all companies of Foot. For example, after the reduction of the old London Trained Bands due to their questionable loyalty to the new regime in 1650, new 'London Volunteer Regiments' were raised by the Commonwealth. An order for 28th August 1650 detailed some of their equipment as '1,000 matchlock muskets, 500 snaphance muskets, 500 pikes, 1,500 bandoliers and 2,000 swords'. One might speculate that the high proportion of firelocks were to guard the Tower with its magazine of powder. Further, one of the first campaigns of the Protectorate Army during the 1650s forcefully demonstrated the important role of firelocks in outpost and irregular warfare in the suppression of Glencairn's Royalist uprising in Scotland in 1654. In a letter to General George Monck in early 1654, Colonel Robert Lilburne stressed the need for 'some more firelocks' to help counter the Highlanders' guerrilla tactics. The operational advantages of the firelock, with its instant readiness for action and the fact it did not give away the presence of its holder, being at a premium.

That the use of firelocks was increasing throughout the period was also demonstrated by the fact that the production of such weapons dramatically increased. While the records for the Royalists Ordnance office were inconclusive in this respect, those for Parliament's were not. The records for the gunmakers William and John Watson are complete for the whole period 1642-1651 and demonstrate a tremendous increase in the proportion of firelocks being manufactured relative to matchlocks.

The Watson family were central to Parliament's

manufacture of firearms. The period 1642 to early 1645 witnessed the significant importation of Continental weapons, especially from Holland, to make up for shortages. But from early 1645, domestic production for Parliament largely took over, especially from the London Gunmakers Company based just outside the Tower in the Minories. Formed in 1637 it consisted of 53 gunsmiths who were Freeman of London and 62 who were not. Between them they were able to manufacture literally thousands of weapons a month if required and one of the largest manufacturers was the Watson family and in 1646 William Watson became Master Gunmaker and Proofmaster to the Ordnance itself.

By breaking down into three separate periods the Watson's delivery of weapons, the vast increase in the use of the firelock becomes obvious along with the decline in the unit cost of manufacture. It should be noted that in these orders, the contemporary term still used was 'snaphance' although by 1642 all weapons labelled snaphance were recognisably firelocks of either the 'English Lock' or 'Dog Lock' variety.

(1) March 1642 to December 1644, 400 'Muskets with snaphance locks and bandoleers' at 20s each (matchlocks were then 16s each).

(2) January 1645 to June 1646, 2,300 'snaphance muskets to be English full bore and proofe' at an average cost of 15s.6d each (matchlocks were then 11s each).

(3) July 1646 to September 1651, 4,463 snaphance muskets, ranging in price from 12s each in November 1646 to 15s each in October 1647. Of these, 900 were for the navy and 3,563 for the army. In addition, on 17th September 1650 they delivered '400 Snaphance Dragoons' at 13s each. The price of traditional matchlocks also continued to decline during this five year period, the Watson's delivering some 5,000 matchlock muskets for as little as 10s each. The Watson's also supplied flints, for example, on 9th December 1650, 'Flint stones for snaphance muskets and pistolls 12000 at 23s.4d per thousand'.

As demonstrated by these statistics, by the latter period 50% of the Watson's output were firelocks, just short of 5,000 in total as compared with just 400 at the commencement of the war.

While the Watsons were the largest single company, there were others adding to this total. For

The English Foot at Dunbar, 3 September 1650.

Equalled only by Worcester a year later, Cromwell's most complete victory was over the Scots at the Battle of Dunbar on 3 September 1650. In the plate oppposite, Cromwell's foot are beginning to resemble the British thin red line of later centuries. With upwards of twenty percent of musketeers armed with firelocks by 1650, they have doubled their files to be three deep and are delivering a single devastating blast of fire. Generally equipped to a standard pattern, there are few distinctions amongst these soldiers of England's first standing army. Due to changes in civilian fashion, their breeches are now open kneed, otherwise they appear much as a soldier from the First Civil War with broad brimmed hats, bandoliers, pattern swords and snapsacks. Scottish casualties from earlier volleys lay in the foreground in their distinctive hoddon-grey suits and blue bonnets. Otherwise the Scots infantry were equipped to a similar standard and pattern as their English counterparts. Painting by Christa Hook.

example, on 12th March 1652 the Committee of the Ordnance placed an enormous order for the Commonwealth Navy for 5000 matchlocks and 2000 snaphance muskets, along with 1500 pairs of pistols. This order was divided between fifty-eight gunsmiths of the London company and was fully delivered within eight weeks, Robert Murden's share being 50 matchlocks and 30 snaphance muskets, and 30 pairs of pistols, while Ralph Venn's share was 150 matchlocks and 40 snaphance muskets, and 25 pairs of pistols. The Watson's only supplied 150 matchlocks and 60 snaphance muskets, and 35 pairs of pistols for this particular order. It is therefore easy to measure the substantial and sophisticated manufacturing capacity which had evolved in response to the demands of the preceding decade by the mid-1650s even for the supposedly complex mechanism of the firelock.

The Caribbean, 1655

Whilst the nature of irregular warfare dramatically promoted the firelock towards becoming the main firearm of the infantry, England's first standing army engaged in two conflicts in the mid and late 1650s, the style of which were to become the norm for generations of subsequent English soldiers.

Undoubtedly the most exotic theatre of conflict was that of the Caribbean where for the first, but certainly not the last time, an English army conducted a colonial campaign. Cromwell, having become Lord Protector in December 1653, immediately used his unrivalled power to bring to an end the war with the Dutch. Cromwell viewed foreign policy, not through the eyes of a mid-seventeenth century merchant eager

The heat of the Caribbean has ensured this English musketeer is lightly clothed, although he is otherwise equipped to European standards. Partizan Press.

Like his musketeer comrade, this pikeman makes do with shirt sleeve order although he does wear a short sleeveless leather waistcoat. Partizan Press.

for commercial advantage, but as a Tudor Puritan continuing the war against the evil Papists. Cromwell thus determined upon a war with Spain. While the traditional theatre of Anglo-Spanish conflict was Flanders and the high seas, Cromwell decided the war should be waged in the Caribbean to seize Spain's immensely wealthy colonies there. Convinced that the cause of Protestantism would be immeasurably strengthened by the seizure of Spain's American gold and silver mines, and riding a wave of popular support for such a conflict, without formally declaring war English warships under Admiral Blake were ordered to commence hostilities in the Caribbean. Meanwhile, in July 1654 the Council of State approved preparations for the 'especial design', namely the dispatch of a military expedition to attack and seize the Spanish Main. Responsibility for this force was given to Major-General Robert Venables with specific orders to begin his attack on Hispaniola (Puerto Rico).

Rather than assigning existing regiments, Venables' army was raised by drafts from the regular army in England and from volunteers, motivated by stories of

Spanish riches. Neither source provided soldiers of quality, in fact it was quite the reverse. The naive expectation had been that Venables' regiments would receive soldiers who had freely volunteered from the existing regiments. Instead, any such individuals were dissuaded and even punished by their officers. Rather colonels seized the opportunity to purposely draft only their very worst soldiers. Only the dregs of each regiment were despatched, armed and equipped with the worst each regiment had. Venables himself commented that amongst these drafts were 'diverse Papists, in particular Sixteen, and four of them Irish, and one a Priest, were put upon us out of the Tower Regiment: many more were found since, though all we could discover were cashired at Barbadoes'. In the event only 1,000 men were drafted from the regular army, the balance being made up by beating for 1,000 plus recruits on the streets of London. The quality of such recruits was abysmal, 'Drums were also beaten up for such voluntary soldiers as were willing to serve the commonwealth beyond sea; which gave encouragement to several who go by the name of

hectors, and knights of the blade, with common cheats, thieves, cutpurses, and such like lewd persons, who had long time lived by the slight of hand, and dexterity of wit, and were now making a fair progress unto Newgate, from whence they were to proceed towards Tyburn; but, considering the dangerousness of that passage, very politicly directed their course another way, and became soldiers for the state. Some sloathful and thievish servants likewise, to avoid the punishment of the law, and coveting a yet more idle life followed after in the same path; there were also drawn forth, out of most of the old standing regiments, such as were newly enlisted, to complete the number. For those who were better prinipled, and knew what fighting was, were (it would seem) reserved for a better purpose, some few only excepted; which were as a mixture of little wine with much water, the

128 New Styles of Warfare 1646-60

French flint-lock pistol c.1650-60. The Trustees of the Wallace Collection, A1208.

one losing its proper strength and vigour, and the other thereby little bettered'.

Having drafted and beaten up a total of at most 2,500 men in London during November 1654, they were organised into five regiments of foot, Robert Venables', James Heane's, Richard Fortescue's, Anthony Buller's and Andrew Carter's, one troop of horse and a small artillery train. Although Venables asked for time to train his men, the Council of State demanded an immediate departure and the entire body were embarked at Portsmouth by late December. The expedition then sailed to the English West Indies, described as 'the dunghill whereon England doth cast forth its rubbish'. Arriving at Barbados in late January after a rapid five week crossing, a further 3,400 islanders were raised, including a sixth regiment under Lieutenant-Colonel Edward O'Doyley. A seventh regiment, numbering 1,200 men, was recruited on St.Christopher by Colonel Richard Holdcp. These

Opposite.

A heavy close-helmet of 'Savoyard' type, for siege warfare, North Italian c.1635. The Trustees of the Wallace Collection, A180.

colonists were mostly impressed servants who were inevitably lacking in both enthusiasm and even the basics of military training. As the original troop of horse had been driven by contrary winds into Ireland and was not to arrive until after the seizure of Jamaica, Venables also raised two fresh troops of horse in Barbados totalling some 143 officers and men. The final military formation to be raised was the 1,200 strong Sea Regiment under Colonel, Vice-Admiral William Goodson. Composed of sailors from the navy and officered by captains from ships of the fleet it was one of the first marine regiments of its kind. Ultimately, Venables departed Barbados in March 1655 for Hispaniola with a numerically respectable force of just over 9,000 men.

Although the largest colonial expedition to have been dispatched by England to that date and with £30,000 allocated to cover its immediate costs, it was a far from satisfactory force. This unruly, largely untrained and rapidly thrown together army of doubtful draftees, adventurers and colonists, lacked any esprit de corps. To cement these woeful inadequacies its standard of equipment and clothing left much to be desired. Although a considerable proportion of the troops were drafted from the standing army few had serviceable equipment, 'almost

Detail of the lock on the French flint-lock pistol c.1650-60 The Trustees of the Wallace Collection, A1208.

half their arms were defective and altogether unserviceable'. Consequently, retaining the established 2:1 ratio of shot to pike, some 4,000 muskets and bandoleers were issued from the Tower, 1,000 of which were 'snaphance' along with ten tons of 'flint stones', purchased at 13s 4d per thousand. It was probable that one company in each of the six infantry regiments were armed with firelocks as certainly, in General Venables own regiment, Captain Pawley or Pawlet's were so armed. There was also a specific company of firelocks attached to the train of artillery under the command of Captain Johnson which had a strength of 12 officers and 120 men. In addition, 3,000 powder bags were issued 'in leure of ye 4,000 [powder] hornes formerly Ordered for ye present Expedition'. As this total of firearms was inadequate to arm all the shot ultimately raised after arrival in Barbados, over 300 miscellaneous private weapons were seized from the islanders. The Tower also issued 2,000 long pikes and 1,000 half-pikes. The issue of these shorter pikes reflected an appreciation of the dense vegetation to be expected and ultimately all pikemen appear to have been issued them as a further 2,500 ten foot long half

pikes were manufactured in Barbados. Other weapons from the Tower included 250 carbines for the troop of horse accompanying the expedition, for which 100 backs, breasts and helmets, 150 pairs of pistols and holsters and 250 saddles were also issued. Whilst not specifically identified as a unit, the 250 'Dragoone peeces' issued, probably equipped dismounted dragoons used for scouting, the 50 fowling pieces '4 Or 5 foote' in length being for the 60 'foot-troopers' of the Scout Master General's company.

Finally, expecting mainly siege operations once through the jungle, a small artillery train was issued, including three mortars, four heavy guns and six field pieces or 'drakes'. As with so much that went wrong with this expedition, only one mortar and two drakes actually arrived. Originally allocated to guard the artillery, its company of firelocks under Captain Johnson were instead employed with their infantry counterparts shielding the army's flank as it struggled through the dense foliage of Hispaniola.

Apart from the critical shortage of weapons, the most crucial omission was a complete failure to supply

Opposite.

Silver-encrusted English 'hunting' hanger hilt c.1640-50. The Trustees of the Wallace Collection, A718.

water bottles, an astonishing situation given the known stifling heat of this theatre of war.

With such poor quality troops and lacking adequate equipment for a tropical campaign, it is surprising Venables achieved anything. In the early stages of the campaign Captain Pawlet commanded a specific force of firelocks which operated in text-book fashion. With the very first landing on 14th April 1655, on the Spanish Island of Hispaniola, Captain Pawlet's firelocks formed part of the scouting force. According to a contemporary account, there were 'Captain Pawlet's firelocks on both wings in the woods to discover ambuscados'. Pawlet's firelocks continued to operate as part of the advance guard, scouting ahead of the main force until largely destroyed on 25th April before the City of San Domingo. Although the rest of the expedition was comprehensively defeated outside the City of San Domingo, the depleted expedition went on to successfully conquer the almost undefended island of Jamaica a few weeks later. This initiated what would ultimately become Britain's substantial Caribbean empire.

Flanders, 1657-60

Whilst the war in the Caribbean was swamped and bitten to death, 1657 found the war with Spain moving to the far more familiar flatlands of Flanders and a far more conventional style of conflict. Against the background of the Anglo-Spanish war in March 1657, an Anglo-French treaty was signed committing England to furnish 6,000 infantry divided into six regiments of 1,000 men each to fight alongside the French in Flanders.

This was the first major field army for what might be termed a conventional theatre of war fielded by England since September 1651 at Worcester. It was stipulated that they were all to be Englishmen with no Scots or Irish. Having recruited new soldiers from the streets, some 1,475 men were drawn from ten existing regiments of foot to complete the 6,000 required. Sir John Reynolds having initially been placed in command, the six colonels were himself, Thomas Morgan, Roger Alsop, Samuel Clark, Sir Bryce Cochrane (ironically a Scots officer) and Henry Lillingston. On 5th May 1657, Reynolds' men were directed to receive 'red coats and shoes when they are ready'. This was followed on 4th August by a contract with Sir John Reynolds, whereby Major Robert Cobbett was to provide 6,000 red cloth coats at 9s each for his soldiers, and 4 grey coats for the Marshal-General's men at £5 each at a total cost of £2,720. Rather uniquely, although the regiments at the end of the first Civil War had been reducing the proportion

of pikemen, due to the French army having a ratio of 1:1, it was originally intended that Reynold's infantry would be armed to a matching ratio. In the event a more standard ratio of 2:1 was adopted, the Ordnance Office at the Tower ordering in April the delivery of 2,000 matchlock muskets, 1,000 pikes and '3,000 swords or rapiers, and 3000 belts' for 3,000 newly raised troops.

Reynold's command appears to have been generally of a sound quality in marked contrast to the forces dispatched to the Caribbean. Many of his officers were veterans as were a considerable proportion of the rank and file. Inevitably supplies and replacements for campaign losses from England were inadequate and returning to England in December in an attempt to sort matters out Reynolds was drowned. Sir William Lockhart took command and it was under his command that these men stormed to victory in the Battle of the Dunes on 4th June 1658. Here, the Protectorate's soldiers played the crucial role in defeating a combined Spanish-English Royalist army in what was in many ways the last battle of the English Civil War. As was becoming the norm, firelocks were to the fore.

Whilst there were no specific surviving warrant for the issue of firelocks to the infantry, two contemporary accounts by the senior officers of that force gave prominence to Lockhart's force having a body of 400 firelocks. The first related how some detachments of picket foot (firelocks) were sent out to be stationed amongst the squadrons of French horse on the right wing. These 'four hundred firelocks' were then recalled and ordered to take part in an attack on a strongly defended sand-hill on the right wing of the Anglo-French army. He related how the body of firelocks fired on two sides of this sand-hill which was inaccessible to assault whilst two infantry regiments assaulted its front. Then the firelocks supported Lockhart's own Blue Regiment's assault on the Spanish front which won the day. A second account, by Major-General Sir Thomas Morgan, supports this and gives further details. He initially places them on 'the right wing with the Blue Regiment, and the 400 Firelocks which were in the intervals of the French Horse'. Then, supported by the Blue and the White regiments, 'the 400 Firelocks shock the enemy's right wing off the ground'. Finally, Morgan ordered 'the Blue Regiment and the 400 Firelocks to advance to the Charge'.

Both Lockhart's and Morgan's accounts made it clear that the firelocks operated as a specific unit on the field of battle. Their total number equated to the 75 odd firelocks (each company having a file of such) one would have expected to find in each of the six regiments of foot and it would seem fair to conclude that the firelocks of each regiment had been temporarily drawn together as the battle commenced. This practice appears to foreshadow the later 1670s and 80s practice of forming the grenadier files from each of the ten companies of a battalion into a single formation for combat (seperate grenadier companies did not exist in the English army until the start of the eighteenth century). Interestingly, the initial deployment of the firelocks in the intervals between the French squadrons of horse recalled Prince Rupert's deployment of commanded shot in the intervals amongst the Royalist horse at Naseby.

Receiving the coastal town of Dunkirk as a prize, a considerable proportion of Lockhart's troops were still its garrison at the Restoration in May 1660. Remaining there for some time, a considerable body of these veterans of the Protectorate, mostly Colonel Henry Lillingston's regiment, were ultimately shipped off to re-enforce the garrison of Tangiers. Thus, alongside General Monck's Regiment (half of whose companies had originally been Walter Lloyd's regiment in Essex's army before the New Model amalgamation in 1645), they bridged the gap between the old and new standing armies, becoming respectively the 2nd (the Queen's) Regiment of Foot and the Coldstream Guards.

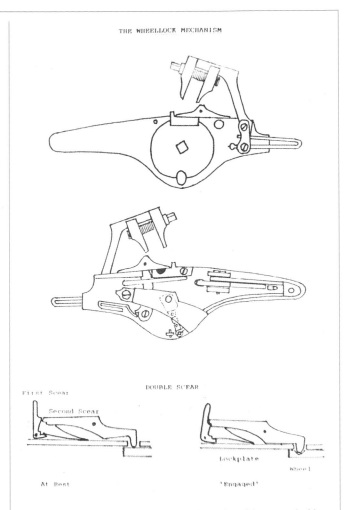

THE WHEELLOCK MECHANISM

DOUBLE SCEAR

First Scear

Second Scear

Lockplate

Wheel

At Post

'Engaged'

Whilst less than reliable, many pistols and carbines carried by harquebusiers were complex wheelocks, requiring 'spanning' (literally winding up) before action. Partizan Press.

Bibliography

John Adair, *Cheriton 1644*, 1973.

John Adair, *By the Sword Divided*, (London 1983).

Richard Atkyns, *The Vindication of Richard Atkyns* (in *Military Memoirs: the Civil War*, ed. Peter Young) (London 1967).

William Barriffe, *Military Discipline: or the young artilleryman*, (1635 &1661).

Captain John Bingham, *The Tactiks of Aelian*, (1616).

Captain John Bingham, *The Art of Embattailing an Army, or The Second Part of Aelians Tacticks*, (London 1629).

This veteran drummer of the recreated Fairfax Battalia beats the order received from his officer. English Heritage.

David Blackmore, *Arms & Armour of the English Civil Wars*, (Royal Armouries 1990).

Richard Brezinski, *The Army of Gustavus Adolphus, Infantry*, (Osprey 1991).

Richard Brezinski, *The Army of Gustavus Adolphus, Cavalry*, (Osprey 1993).

Nathaneal Burt, *Militarie Instructions, or The Souldier tried for the use of the Dragoon*, (Wapping 1644).

Calender of State Papers Domestic.

Edward Hyde, Earl of Clarendon, *History of the Rebellion and Civil Wars in England*, ed. W.D.Macray (Oxford 1888).

John S.Cooper, *For Commonwealth and Crown*, (Wilson Hunt 1993).

John Cruso, *Militarie Instructions for the Cavallerie*, (Cambridge1632).

Jacob De Gheyn, *Wapenhandelinghe van Roers Musquetten Ende Spiessen*, (Holland 1607).

William Eldred, *The Gunners Glasse*, (London 1646).

Richard Elton, *The Compleat Body of the Art Military*, (London 1650).

English Civil War Notes & Queries: Partizan Press, Various issues

James Ferguson, *Papers Illustrating the History of The Scots Brigade in the service of the United Netherlands 1572-1782*, 3 Vols. (Scottish History Society, Edinburgh 1899-1901).

Sir Charles Firth, *The Clarke Papers*, 4 Vols. (Camden Society 1891-1901).

Sir Charles Firth (ed), *Memoirs of Edmund Ludlow*, 2 Vols. (Clarendon Press 1894).

Sir Charles Firth (ed), *The Narrative of General Venables*, (Camden Society 1900).

Sir Charles Firth, *Cromwell's Army*, (Greenhill re-print 1992).

Sir Charles Firth, *The Battle of Dunbar*, (Vol.XIV, Transactions of the Royal Historical Society).

Sir Charles Firth & Godfrey Davies, *Regimental History of Cromwell's Army*, (2 Vols., Oxford 1940).

Mark C.Fissel, *The Bishops' Wars*, (Cambridge

University Press 1994).

Sir J.W.Fortescue, *History of the British Army*, Vol.I, (London 1899).

James Hall (ed) *Memorials of the Civil War in Cheshire and the Adjacent Counties, Thomas Malbon of Nantwich, Gent,* (1889).

Henry Hexham, *Principles of the Art Military; practised in the Warres of the United Netherlands,* (London 1637 and extended second edition 1642).

Gervase Holles, *Memorials of the Holles Family 1493-1656,* (Camden Third Series Vol.LV, 1937).

Clive Holmes, *The Eastern Association in the English Civil War,* (Cambridge 1974).

Lucy Hutchinson, *Memoirs of the Life of Colonel Hutchinson,* Sir Charles Firth (ed.), (Clarendon Press 1885).

Ronald Hutton, *The Royalist war effort 1642-1646,* (Longman 1981).

Dr. Peter Krenn, *Test-Firing Selected 16th-18th Century Weapons,* translated by Dr.Erwin Schmidl, Military Illustrated, no.33, February 1991.

Cecil C.P.Lawson, *The Uniforms of the British Army,* Vol.1, (London 1940).

John Lowe, *The Campaign of the Irish Royalist Army in Cheshire, November 1643-January 1644,* (Vol.III, Transactions of the Historic Society of Lancashire and Cheshire, 1959).

Sir Samuel Luke, *Journal of Sir Samuel Luke,* I.G.Philip (ed), 3 Vols., Oxfordshire Record Society, 1947, 1950 and 1950-53.

Sir Samuel Luke, *The Letter Books of Sir Samuel Luke, 1644-45,* H.G.Tibbutt (ed), Joint publication of the Bedfordshire Historical Record Society and HMC 1963.

Clements R. Markham, *The Fighting Veres,* (London 1888).

Francis Markham, *Five Decades of Epistles of Warre,* (London 1622).

Gervase Markham, *The Souldiers Accidence,* (London 1625).

George Monck, *Observations upon Military and Political Affairs,* (London 1671).

Gerald Mungeam, *Contracts for the Supply of Equipment to the New Model Army in 1645,* Journal of the Arms and Armour Society, VI, (1968).

Roger, Earl of Orrery, *A Treatise of the Art of War,* (London 1677).

Dr.Geoffrey Parker, *The Army of Flanders and the Spanish Road 1567-1659,* (Cambridge University Press1972).

Dr. Geoffrey Parker, *The Military Revolution, 1560-1660-a myth?,* Journal of Modern History, XLVII (1976).

Dr.Geoffrey Parker, *The Military Revolution: Military Innovation and the Rise of the West,* (Cambridge 1988).

Stuart Peachey & Les Prince, *ECW Flags and Colours: English Foot,* (Partizan Press 1991).

Stuart Peachey and Alan Turton, *Common Soldiers Clothing of the Civil Wars 1639-1646, Volume 1 Infantry,* (Stuart Press 1995).

Stuart Peachey & Alan Turton, *Old Robin's Foot,* (Partizan Press 1987).

Edward Peacock, *The Army Lists of the Roundheads and Cavaliers,* (2nd ed. London 1874).

J.R.Philips, *Memoirs of the Civil War in Wales and the Marches,* 2 Vols. (London 1874).

MSS of the Duke of Portland at Welbeck, Historical Manuscripts Commission, 1893.

Instructions For Musters And Armes, And the use thereof: By order from the Lords of His Maiesties most Honourable Privy Counsayle 1623.

Directions for Musters, 1638.

The Exercise of the English in the Militia of the Kingdome of England, (1641).

Military Orders And Articles Established by His Majestie, (1642 & 1643).

G.A.Raikes, *History of the Honourable Artillery Company,* (London 1878).

Stuart Reid, *Gunpowder Triumphant,* (Partizan Press 1987).

Stuart Reid, *Covenanters: Scots Infantry in the 1640's,* Military Illustrated, no.19, June/July 1989.

Keith Roberts, *Soldiers of the English Civil War (1): Infantry,* (Osprey 1989).

Dr. Ian Roy, *The Royalist Army in the First Civil War,* (Unpublished Phd. thesis 1963).

Dr. Ian Roy, *The Royalist Ordnance Papers, 1642-1646,* Parts I and II, (Oxfordshire Record Societ, 1964 and 1978).

Ian Ryder, *An English Army for Ireland,* (Partizan Press 1987).

Sir Sibbald David Scott, *The British Army, its Origin, Progress and Equipment,* (London 1868).

Josiah Sprigge, *Anglia Rediviva: England's Recovery,* (London, 1647).

Paul Sutton, *Cromwell's Jamaica Campaign,* (Partizan Press 1990).

Richard Symonds, *Diary of the Marches of the Royal Army,* C.E.Long (ed) (Camden Society 1859).

John Tincey, *Soldiers of the English Civil War (2): Cavalry,* (Osprey 1990).

Thomason Tracts, British Library.

Margaret Toynbee & Peter Young, *Cropredy Bridge, 1644,* (Kineton 1970).

Margaret Toynbee & Peter Young, *Strangers in Oxford,*

(Kineton 1973).

Sir James Turner, *Pallas Armata: Militarie Essayes of the Ancient Grecian, Roman and Modern Art of War*, (London 1683).

Alan Turton, *The Chief Strength of the Army, Essex's Horse (1642-1645)*, (Partizan Press 1992).

Captain Thomas Venn, *Military & Maritine Discipline in Three Books*, (London 1672).

John Vernon, *The young Horse-man, or the honest plain-dealing Cavalier*, (London 1644).

Sir Edward Walker, *Historical Discourses*, (1705).

Johann Jacobi von Wallhausen, *Kriegskunst zu Fuss*, (Oppenheim1615).

Johann Jacobi von Wallhausen, *Manuale Militare, Oder Krieggs Manual*, (Frankfurt-am-Main 1616).

Colonel Clifford Walton, *History of the British Standing Army*, 1894.

Edward E.G.Warburton, *Memorials of Prince Rupert and the Cavaliers*, 3 Vols. (Bentley 1849).

Robert Ward, *Animadversions of Warre*, (London 1639).

Peter Wenham, *The Great and Close Siege of York*, (Kineton 1970).

Nehemiah Wharton, *The Edgehill Campaign & the letters of Nehemiah Wharton*, Stuart Peachey (ed) (Partizan Press 1989).

Bulstrode Whitelocke, *Memorials of the English Affairs*, (Oxford University Press 1853).

Anthony Wood, *The Life and Times of Anthony Wood, antiquary, of Oxford*, 1632-1695, 5 Vols. (Oxford Histotical Society 1891).

Norah Waugh, *The Cut of Men's Clothes, 1600-1900*, (London 1964).

Russell F. Weigley, *The Age of Battles*, (Indiana University Press1991).

Peter Young and Wilfrid Embleton, *The Cavalier Army: Its Organization and Everyday Life*, (Allen & Unwin 1974).

Peter Young, *Edgehill 1642*, (Kineton 1967).

Peter Young, *Marston Moor*, (Kineton 1970).

Peter Young, *Naseby*, (Century Publishing1985).

English Civil War Directory

Museums and Collections

The Royal Armouries Museum,
Armouries Drive, Leeds, LS10 1LT.
Tel:0113-220-1999.
Open seven days a week, 10-5.
The new purpose built museum in Leeds contains numerous pieces of armour, arms and equipment dating from the English Civil War and has the closest to what one might describe as a comprehensive collection of the period.

The Wallace Collection,
Hertford House, Manchester Square, London, WIM 6BN.
Tel: 0171-935-0687.
Open seven days a week, 10-5.
This has the second largest collection of arms and armour of the period, although predominantly of Continental manufacturer.

National Army Museum,
Royal Hospital Road, Chelsea, London, SW3.
Tel: 0171-730-0717.
Open seven days a week, 10-5.
This has a limited number of firearms and swords of the English Civil War alongside various miscellaneous items of equipment including some fine buff-coats.

Gunnersbury Park Museum,
Gunnersbury Park, W3,
Tel:0181-992-2248.
Often neglected, this has the world's largest collection of contemporary Jencks swords, including many rare soldiers pattern versions of both the infantry and cavalry.

Worcester Armoury,
Worcester.
Although a limited quantity of original items, it is an interesting centre to gain an introduction to the period and for an account of Worcester's varied experiences during the conflict.

Oliver Cromwell's House,
Ely, Cambridgeshire.
Tel: 01353-662062.
Provides an insight into the domestic, military and political aspects of Cromwell's life and times.

Cromwell Museum,
Huntingdon.
A fascinating collection of both Cromwell's personal items and much else general to the period.

The Cromwell Association,
Cosswell Cottage, Northedge, Tupton, Chesterfield, Derbyshire, S42 6AY.
The Cromwell Association seeks to promote and encourage interest in Oliver Cromwell, the English Civil War, the Commonwealth and the Protectorate.

Re-enactment Societies

The English Civil War period is easily the largest section of the British re-enactment scene and contains many varied groups, ranging from several thousand members nationwide to small local groups of just a few dozen.

The oldest and largest of the societies is the Sealed Knot with over 6,000 members, staging a comprehensive programme of battle re-enactment and living history displays each year. To contact the SK write to: The Sealed Knot Society Ltd, PO. Box 2000, Nottingham, NG2 5LS or telephone, 01384-295939.

The English Civil War Society is of similar long standing and sub-divided into the Roundhead Association and the King's Army. As with the SK they mount a substantial programme of battle and living history events each year. To contact the King's Army write to: 70 Hailgate, Howden, North Humberside, DN14 7ST or telephone 01430-430695. To contact the Roundhead Association write to: 149, Gillot Road, Edgebaston, Birmingham, B16 OET or telephone 0121-4550062.

The Siege Group is primarily a living history society, although it does stage small skirmishes and sieges. To contact the SG write to: Flat 11, Marlborough Court, Marlborough Hill, Harrow, Middlesex, HA1 1UF or telephone, 0181-861-0830.

Re-enactment Suppliers and Bookshops

The best way to gain access to the many dozens of excellent suppliers of English Civil war re-enactment clothes and equipment is to join one of the societies and take advantage of 'merchants row'. The following are just a handful of the suppliers chosen at random and their listing does not indicate preference.

Ages of Elegance and Military Metalwork.
480, Chiswick High Road, London, W4 5TT.
Tel: 0181-742-0730.
High quality reproduction clothing, specialising in civilian and military clothing, linen armour, gloves, lacework, embroidery and headwear. Also metal and leather military accoutrements plus living history items.

Armour Class,
193a Dumbarton Road, Clydebank, Glasgow, G81 4XJ.
Tel: 0141-951-2262.
Suppliers of reproduction/re-enactment weapons & armour.

Bailiff Forge,
Unit 53, Colne Valley Workshops, Linthwaite, Huddersfield, HD7 5QG.
Tel: 01484-846973.
Manufactures swords, armour and accessories.

Bodgerarmour,
The East Barn, Moulton St Mary, Norwich, Norfolk, NG13 3NQ.
Tel: 01493-751756.
Superb quality manufacturer of weapons, cutlery and living history items in general.

Caliver Books,
816-818, London Road, Leigh-on-Sea, Essex, SS9 3NH.
Tel: 01702-73986.
Undoubtedly the most comprehensive listing of all written works on the ECW.

Civil Wardrobe,
Newtown Road, Newbury, Berks, RG14 7ER.
Tel: 01635-43806.
Suppliers of seventeenth century clothing, leatherwork and accessories.

The Drop Spindle,
35, Cross Street, Upton, Pontefract, WF9 1EU.
Tel: 01977-647647.
Suppliers of seventeenth century costume and spinning supplies.

English Armourie,
Dept.10, 1 Walsall Street, Willenhall, W.Mids, WV13 2EX.
Tel: 01902-870579.
Supplier of steel armour, matchlocks, doglocks and all contemporary shooting accessories.

English Civil War Shoes,
Pinnocks Farm, Northmoor, Witney, Oxon, OX8 1AY.
Tel: 01865-300626.
Supplies both open-sided latchet shoes and closed-in sided soldiers' shoes.

Marcus Music,
Tredegar House, Newport, Gwent.
Tel: 01633-815612
Makers and repairers of early musical instruments, including Civil War drums.

Paul Meekins,
34, Townsend Road, Tiddington, Stratford-upon-Avon, Warwickshire, CV37 7DE.
Tel: 01789-295086.
Stockists of English Civil War books and 17th century books in general.

The Two 'J's'.
32 Ashfield Drive, Anstey, Leicester, LE7 7TA.
Tel: 01533-363514.
Manufacturers of swords, baldricks, polearms and leatherwork.

Past Tents,
High View Bungalow, Main Street, Clarborough, Retford, Notts., DN22 9NJ.
Tel: 01777-869821.
Manufactures high quality, reproduction tents for all historical periods.

Sarah Juniper, Cordwainer,
109, Woodmancote, Dursley, Gloucestershire, GL11

4AH.
Tel: 01453-545675.
Maker of high quality handsewn boots and shoes.

Victor James,
15 Whitmore Road, Chaddesden, Derby, DE21 6HR.
Tel: 01332-663432.
Manufacturer of re-enactment equipment, including
baldricks, scabbards, belts and tents, works in metal,
wood, canvas and leather.

Yorkshire Historic Arms,
14 Anvil Street, Brighouse, West Yorkshire, HD6 1TP.
Tel: 01484-716130.
Manufactures muskets, musketeers' equipment and
pewterware.

English Civil War Art

The Historic Art Company, Ashleigh House, 236
Wokingham Road, Reading, Berks RG6 IJS publishes
English Civil War prints by Chris Collingwood, one
of Britain's leading military artists. Collingwood has
illustrated a broad range of periods, but has a
particular affinity for the Civil War. His work is
thoroughly researched and the figures in his paintings
have a real flair and capture all the tragedy and
romance of the turbulent period.

Collingwood's work includes individual portraits of
Civil War soldiers and group scenes. The individual
prints feature a pikeman of the King's Lifeguard and a
musketeer of the Earl of Manchester's Regiment.
Panoramic action paintings include *For God and
Parliament*, depicting Parliamentarian troopers in a
spirited charge, and *For Sack and Plunder* depicting
wealthy householders being rescued from robbers by
the timely arrival of a group of King's Horse.
Collingwood's most famous print is *For King and
Kingdom*, depicting Royalist troops during the early
stages of the war preparing for battle. Chris will also
accept private commissions for Civil War art.

Cranston Fine Arts, Torwood House, Torwoodhill
Road, Rhu, Helensburgh G84 8LE, Scotland (Tel
01436 820269, Fax: 01436 820473) offers a selection of
fine English Civil War prints by Ernest Crofts. Crofts
had a fine romantic style and Cranston's selection of
his work includes *Advance Guard of the New Model
Army*, *Charles I On His Way To Execution* and *Funeral of
Charles 1, St George's Chapel, Windsor*. Cranston also
offer a print of Sir John's Gilbert's painting, *After The
Battle of Naseby*. Military artist Ed Dovey accepts
commissions for English Civil War art including battle
scenes and portraiture. Ed can be contacted at 70
Clement Close, Willesden, London NW6 7AN.

Stephen Beck, former Sergeant Painter to the Sealed
Knot, offers a series of traditional style Civil War
prints, including a new version of The Battle of
Lansdown with an accompanying printed description.
He has also produced prints of Broughton Castle in
the Civil War and the execution of army levellers at
Burford Churchyard on May 17, 1649. Stephen also
designs to order letterheads and decorative notepaper
vignettes. He can be contacted at 6 St Anne's Way,
Bath, Avon BA2 6BT (Tel: 01225 463857).

English Civil War Model Soldiers and Wargames Figures

Although the English Civil War was a colourful period
it has never been an overwhelmingly popular period
with model soldier manaufacturers: but there are some
companies producing excellent work.

Fort Royal Review of 25 Woolhope Road,
Worcester WR5 2AR (Tel: 01905 356379, Fax: 01905
764265) produce a splendid 120mm officer of the New
Model Army 1648. It is hoped that the company will
continue to produce English Civil War figures in its
diverse range of miniatures.

Keith Durham, one of Britain's most talented
sculptors has sculpted an 80mm figure of a musketeer,
New Model Army, at the Battle of Naseby for Border
Miniatures. Durham has depicted the musketeer
shortly before the battle took place, fortifying himself
with a drink from a pewter tankard. The figure is a
very well sculpted piece and Border's range also
includes a mounted trooper of Parliamentary horse
and more English Civil War miniatures are being
planned. Border Miniatures are at Fernlea, Penrith
Road, Keswick, Cumbria CA12 4LJ (Tel/Fax: 017687
71302).

Tradition of London Limited, Britain's long
established model soldier company at 33 Curzon
Street, Mayfair, London WIY 7AE (Tel: 0171-493-
7452, Fax: 0171-365-1224) produce an extensive range
of English Civil War figures. In 54mm scale they have
an officer of the King's Lifeguard, an officer of
artillery, a fifer of infantry, a cuirassier and a trooper of
Parliamentary Horse. In 90mm scale Tradition offers a
musketeer, a cavalry trooper, a cavalry officer and an
infantry officer. Tradition's toy soldier range includes a
trooper of Parliamentary Horse, an officer of Royalist
Foot and a musketeer of the Trained Bands.

Sarum Soldiers of 2a Upper Tooting Park, London
SW17 7SW (Tel: 0181-767-1535, Fax: 0181-672-
5503) produce a musketeer and a pikeman in their
range of English Civil War miniatures. English Civil
War Flat figure enthusiasts are well catered for with
Western Miniatures' range of flat figures including

pikemen, musketeers, and a personality figure of Charles I. Western Miniatures are at 123 Henacre Road, Shirehampton, Bristol, BSll OH6.

Redoubt Enterprises of 49 Channel View Road, Eastbourne, East Sussex, BN22 7LN (Tel: 01323 738022, Fax: 01323 738032) produce a wide range of 25mm English Civil War wargame figures including an extensive range of cannon and gunners. Wargames Foundry of The Foundry, Mount St, New Basford, Nottingham, NG7 7HX (Phone 0115 97 92002, Fax: 0115 97 92209) also do an extensive range of figures from the period. An illustrated catalogue is available for £2.50.

The Guardroom 38 West Street, Dusnstable, Beds, LU6 lTA (Tel: 01582 60641) can supply complete English Civil War armies in 15mm scale using figures produced by Miniature Figurines. Matchlock Miniatures, available from Partizan Press, 816-818 London Road, Leigh-on-Sea Essex, SS9 73986, produce an extensive range of English Civil War wargames figures, including drummers, trumpeters and an extensive selection of cavalry.

English Civil War Books and Magazines

The greatest book source for students of the English Civil War is the range supplied by Caliver Books, who also incorporate Partizan Press and Matchlock Miniatures at 816-818 London Road, Leigh-on-Sea, Essex SS9 3NH (Tel & Fax 01702 73986). They carry a wide range of general and specialist items on uniforms, campaigns and personalities of the Civil War, and have become highly recommended over the years for their fast and friendly service to customers. Partizan Press publishes *English Civil War Times*, the definitive magazine on the period for wargamers, re-enactors and all serious enthusiasts of the Civil War.

Ken Trotman Ltd, Unit 11, 135 Ditton Walk, Cambridge, Cambridgeshire CB5 8QD (Tel: 01223 211030, Fax: 01223 212317) has an extensive range of new and secondhand English Civil War titles by mail order.

Chelifer Books, a mail order business run by Mike Smith from Todd Close, Curthwaite, Wigton, Cumbria (Tel: 01228 711388) carry a range of secondhand books on all aspects of the English Civil War.

Index

Acknowledgements

The writing of this book would not have been possible without the previous research of numerous historians. Firstly my thanks to Keith Roberts for many insights into the relationship between the tactical revolution of the seventeenth century and soldiers' equipment and clothes. For the Royalist Army, Dr. Ian Roy's and John Barrett's research is invaluable, whilst for Parliament, I have drawn heavily on the unparalleled research of Stuart Peachey and Alan Turton, both in terms of clothing generally and for Essex's Army in particular. For the Scots, Stuart Reid's work is yet to be surpassed whilst for the armies in Ireland and the Caribbean, I have drawn heavily upon the work of Ian Ryder and Paul Sutton respectively. For the unfailing generosity and assistance in assembling the pictures which accompany the text my deepest thanks must go to David Edge at the Wallace Collection, Neil Chippendale for the Jencks swords from Gunnersbury Park Museum and Dave Ryan of Partizan Press for certain modern interpretations. For the colour pictures of members of the Fairfax Battalia I am indebted to Howard Giles at English Heritage. Finally, I am grateful to my wife Caz for being persuaded to read my text and correct my many grammatical errors.